Level 2 Diploma for IT Users
for City & Guilds

Level

2

Desktop Publishing

for Office XP

Nicola J Bowman

Endorsed by
City&
Guilds

www.heinemann.co.uk
✓ Free online support
✓ Useful weblinks
✓ 24 hour online ordering

01865 888058

Inspiring generations

Heinemann Educational Publishers
Halley Court, Jordan Hill, Oxford OX2 8EJ
Part of Harcourt Education

Heinemann is the registered trademark of
Harcourt Education Limited

Text © Nicola Bowman 2004

First published 2004

07 06 05 04
10 9 8 7 6 5 4 3 2 1

British Library Cataloguing in Publication Data is available
from the British Library on request.

ISBN 0 435 46250 4

Publisher's note
The materials in this Work have been developed by Harcourt Education and the
content and the accuracy are the sole responsibility of Harcourt Education. The City
and Guilds of London Institute accepts no liability howsoever in respect of any
breach of the intellectual property rights of any third party howsoever occasioned or
damage to the third party's property or person as a result of the use of this Work.

The City & Guilds name and logo are the registered trade marks of the City and
Guilds of London Institute and are used under licence.

Typeset by Tech-Set Ltd, Gateshead, Tyne & Wear
Printed in UK by Thomson Litho

Acknowledgements
The screenshots in this book are reproduced with permission from Microsoft
Corporation.

Tel: 01865 888058 www.heinemann.co.uk

Contents

Introduction

City & Guilds e-Quals is an exciting new range of IT qualifications developed with leading industry experts. These comprehensive, progressive awards cover everything from getting to grips with basic IT to gaining the latest professional skills.

The range consists of both User and Practitioner qualifications. User qualifications (Levels 1–3) are ideal for those who use IT as part of their job or in life generally, while Practitioner qualifications (Levels 2–3) have been developed for those who need to boost their professional skills in, for example, networking or software development.

e-Quals boasts online testing and a dedicated website with news and support materials and web-based training. The qualifications reflect industry standards and meet the requirements of the National Qualifications Framework. With e-Quals you will not only develop your expertise, you will gain a qualification that is recognised by employers all over the world.

This book assumes that you have acquired the skills and knowledge necessary for Desktop Publishing Level 1 and builds on those skills, introducing additional features such as styles, templates and creating your own graphics.

The specific skills and underpinning knowledge for the outcomes of this Desktop Publishing unit are covered, although they are not dealt with separately or in the same order.

Each section covers several practical skills as well as underpinning knowledge related to the unit outcomes. This is followed by skills practice and a chance to check your knowledge. Consolidation tasks give you the opportunity to put together skills and knowledge, and a practice assignment completes your progress towards the actual assignment. Solutions can be found at the back of the book.

Your tutor will give you a copy of the outcomes, as provided by City & Guilds, so that you can sign and date each learning point as you master the skills and knowledge.

In order to give detailed methods for each task it is necessary to refer to a specific desktop publishing application and operating system, though the City & Guilds unit is not specific and can be completed using any desktop publishing package and operating system. This book refers to Microsoft Publishing 2002.

There is often more than one way of carrying out a task in Publisher, e.g. using the toolbar, menu or keyboard. Whilst this book may use one method, there are others, and alternatives are listed at the back in the quick reference guide.

The tasks are designed to be worked through in order, as earlier tasks may be used in later sections. Good luck!

Revise basics

You will learn to

- Access the DTP environment – hardware/software
- Check RAM
- Change page size
- Change page setup and orientation
- Set gutter space
- Create text and image frames
- Set columns
- Add borders
- Insert an image
- Apply text formatting and alignment
- Change resolution and printing the publication

This book assumes that you have already acquired the skills and knowledge for Desktop Publishing Level 1, and as those topics will be familiar to you, you may be given brief reminders rather than full instructions. The Check your knowledge questions at the end of this section and in each of the other sections tests your knowledge in line with the syllabus.

You should already be able to

- load Publisher
- create and set up a new publication
- create text frames
- enter and edit text (insert and delete)
- format text (change font, size, emphasis, alignment)
- select paper size, orientation and margins
- resize text frames
- save and print
- use Save As
- consider the use of fonts
- manipulate graphics
- close publication and Publisher.

Information: Publications

In this section you will revise the basics of setting up a publication and the Desktop Publishing environment, including the hardware and software of a computer which is used whilst creating publications. Publications created here and in other sections may be used in later sections. Do not omit tasks.

Information: Hardware and software

The hardware components of the computer consist of

- keyboard (to enter text)
- mouse (to select icons, menus, highlight and move text)
- monitor (to view your work)
- floppy and hard disk (to store your work)
- CD-ROM (to obtain images)
- printer (to print your work)
- scanner (to capture text and images – this is covered in greater depth on page 54).

The software that you will use is
- desktop publishing software (to create your publication)
- a text editor (to create text files which can be inserted into the publication)
- a graphics editor (to create or edit images before importing into the publication).

Hint:

To check the available RAM, click on **Start**, right-click **My Computer**, click **Properties** and then the **Performance** tab. If the memory shows 30% free or less you should close down any unnecessary files as you may have difficulty producing your publication.

Information: RAM

When creating publications which contain several objects and images you will be using a large amount of the computer's memory which is known as **RAM (Random Access Memory)**. If you don't save your work or the computer crashes then your work will be lost. However, the RAM stores your work until you save it.

Information: Storage space

Desktop publishing files take up large amounts of storage space, usually because of the graphics inserted. You should check that you have sufficient available storage space before starting your publication. If you are working on a network you may have to ask your tutor for guidance. To check storage space on a floppy disk open **Windows Explorer**, right-click **a:\drive**, **Properties**. To check the storage space on your hard disk open **Windows Explorer**, right-click **c:\drive** (or My Documents folder if that is where you are working), **Properties**.

Information: Revise page size and setup

When creating a new publication, pages should be set up as specified in the assignment or to meet your own display requirements.

Publications can be set up and printed on A4 paper. A4 is a size of paper (210 × 297 mm or 297 × 210 mm) and is based on an international standard. The orientation (which way up the paper is) can be either portrait or landscape. Portrait pages are tall with the shortest edge of the paper at the top and landscape pages are wide with the shortest edge at the side.

A4
Portrait
210 × 297 mm

A4
Landscape
297 × 210 mm

The margins on the page can be used as guides to help you place text and images into the publication and help balance the white space around the edge of the page.

Publications can also be produced on A5 paper for producing leaflets, booklets, notepads or advertisement flyers. Custom-size publications can be used and printed on either A4 or A5 paper.

A5
Landscape
210 × 148 mm

A5
Portrait
148 × 210 mm

Custom Size
190 × 200 mm

Information: Paper weights

The weight of paper is measured in grams. Generally, the higher the weight, the better quality the paper is. Newspapers generally weigh between 54 and 60 grams, A4 paper usually weighs 80 grams, although good quality paper weighs 110 grams.

Information: Columns

Publications can display text and images as columns and Microsoft Publisher provides guides to help you do this.

Hint:

You can turn off the Quick Publication Wizard by clicking on **Tools**, **Options**, **User Assistance** and remove the tick from the checkbox **Use Quick Publication Wizard for blank publications**. Click **OK**.

Hint:

Before you start work, you should check the measurement units. You can check this by clicking on **Tools**, **Options**, **Measurement units** and click on centimetres if not already selected. Click **OK**.

Method

1   Load **Publisher**. The Publisher catalogue is displayed – click on the close icon (Figure 1.1). A new blank document should appear. If not, click on the **File** menu and select **New**.

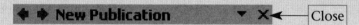

Figure 1.1 New publication

2   Set up a new A4 page to the following specifications – see Figure 1.2 for guidance.

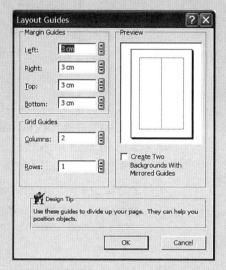

Figure 1.2 Page setup

3   Save the publication as **revise1** and keep the publication open for the next task.

Information: Revise creating text and image frames

All text and images must be placed in text and image frames in Publisher and you will revise how to do this in the next task. In Publisher 2002 text frames are referred to as Text Boxes.

Task 1.2   Create a text frame box

Method

1   Using the publication **revise1**, click on the **Text Box Tool** button in the Object toolbar (Figure 1.3). The pointer changes to a 'crosshair'.

Figure 1.3 Object toolbar

2 Select the **Text Box** tool and position the crosshair in the top left corner of the page on the blue guides.

3 Hold down the left mouse button and drag text box tool from the top left blue line to the bottom right blue line.

4 Save the changes to the publication keeping the filename **revise1** and keep the publication open for the next task.

Information: Revise columns and column spacing

When working with columns, the space between the columns defaults to 0.5 cm in Publisher. The column spacing can be changed by changing the text frame properties or moving the spacing on the ruler.

Task 1.3	Setting two columns and the gutter space

Method

1 Using the publication **revise1**, right-click with the mouse in the text frame area and then select **Format Text Box** from the menu as displayed in Figure 1.4.

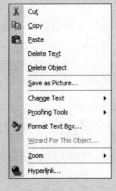

Cut
Copy
Paste
Delete Text
Delete Object
Save as Picture...
Change Text ▶
Proofing Tools ▶
Format Text Box...
Wizard For This Object...
Zoom ▶
Hyperlink...

Figure 1.4 Text box options

2   The dialogue box in Figure 1.5 is now shown.

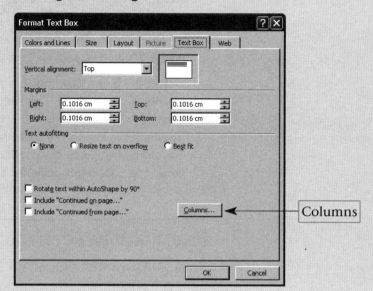

Figure 1.5 Format Text Box

3   Click on **Text Box** and then **Columns** (see Figure 1.6).

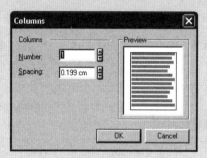

Figure 1.6 Columns dialogue box

4   Change the **Columns**: Number to **2** and Spacing from the default 0.199 cm to **0.4 cm**. The spacing, or gutter, is the distance between the two columns.

5   Save the changes to the publication keeping the filename **revise1** and keep the publication open for the next task.

Hint:

To change the gutter using the rulers, hold down the **Shift** key and position the mouse on the vertical ruler on the left of the window. The pointer changes to the Adjust pointer. Drag the Adjust pointer to 10 cm on the horizontal ruler scale and release. Repeat this process positioning the second guide at 11 cm, leaving a 1 cm gutter.

Information: Revise adding borders

Text and image frames can be enhanced by adding a border. In Publisher you can add different styles of borders and grids as lines, border art or create your own custom borders.

Task 1.4   Adding a border

Method

1 Using the publication **revise1** add a border around both columns as a grid. To do this, right-click with the mouse in the text frame area and then select **Format Text Box** from the menu displayed in Figure 1.4.

2 Click **Colours and Lines**: and choose a black line.

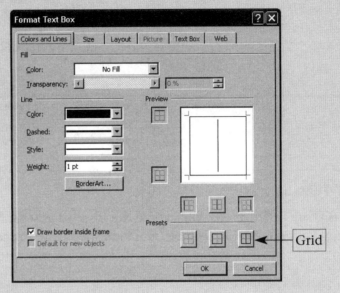

Figure 1.7 Line/Border Style

3 Select **1pt** from the **Line/Weight** box and click **Grid**. Click **OK** (Figure 1.7).

4 Add the following text towards the **bottom of the left column** so that it wraps to the **top of the right column** as shown in the columns layout on page 8. Remember to click in the text frame and when you see the I-beam you are ready to start keying in the text.

Bruno Bear

Invites you to join
Our weekly activities
At Brandon Community Centre

Activities include:

Face Painting
Gym
Free Play
Song time

Note: You will need to enter some blank lines before you start to type. Increase the size of the text so that the lines fill the width of the column.

Add a suitable clip art image

Bruno Bear

Invites you to join

Our weekly activites

At Brandon Community Centre

Activites include:

Face painting

Gym

Free Play

Song time

Insert suitable image

5   Save the publication as **revise1** and keep the publication open for the next task.

Information: Inserting an image

Images that are inserted into publications are inserted as separate objects. The images that you will insert into your publications will be from Publisher's Clip Art gallery.

Task 1.5   Adding an image

Method

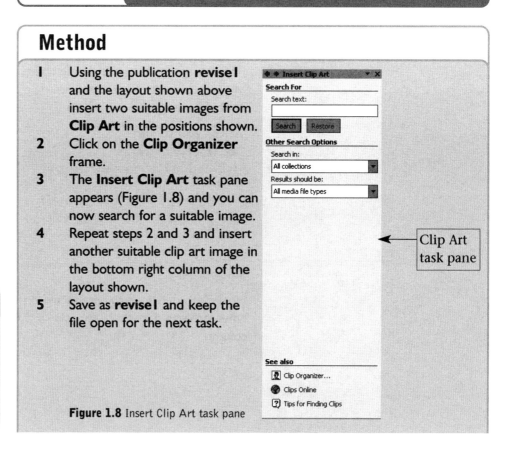

1   Using the publication **revise1** and the layout shown above insert two suitable images from **Clip Art** in the positions shown.

2   Click on the **Clip Organizer** frame.

3   The **Insert Clip Art** task pane appears (Figure 1.8) and you can now search for a suitable image.

4   Repeat steps 2 and 3 and insert another suitable clip art image in the bottom right column of the layout shown.

5   Save as **revise1** and keep the file open for the next task.

Figure 1.8 Insert Clip Art task pane

Hint:

To insert a clip art image relating to bears. In the search box type in **bears** and a selection of clip art images in the bears category will be displayed.

Information: Revise text formatting and alignment

The appearance of text can be changed by altering the font style and the font size. Text can be enhanced by using emphasis, e.g. bold, italics and underline or capitals. Some examples are provided below:

Font	Fonts are usually **sans serif** or **serif** font. A **serif** font means that the characters have curls at the bottom of each character. A **sans serif** font means that characters do not have any curls. The default font in Publisher is usually **Times New Roman**, which is a serif font. **Comic Sans** or **Arial** are examples of sans serif fonts. There are a huge number of fonts available and by using different fonts you can change the tone of your message.
Font size	Publisher's default font size is 10. This is a common body size text. The font size can be changed and increased for headings and subheadings and to highlight key points. This text has been produced in 12 point size. Font size is increased by changing the size to a higher number, e.g. 20 point.
CAPITALS	CAPITALS are commonly used for headings to indicate the highest hierarchy of headings.
Bold	**Bold** makes the text darker and heavier than normal text. Bold can be used to emphasise headings or subheadings or key words in the text.
Italics	*Italics* can be used as another form of emphasis.
<u>Underline</u>	<u>Underline</u> can be used in a subheading style to emphasise where a new section of the document is to start.
Alignment	Alignment of text can be left, right, centred or justified. **Left aligned text starts at the left margin** **Right aligned text starts at the right margin** **Centred text is centred between the left and right margins** **Text which is justified is where the text is evenly aligned between both left and right margins, creating a smooth edge on both the left and right right sides of the text.**

The Formatting toolbar (Figure 1.9) shows the buttons that are required to change the font style, font size and to add emphasis to the text.

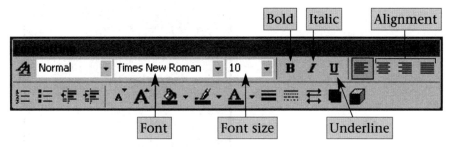

Figure 1.9 Formatting toolbar

Method

1	Highlight the text **Bruno Bear** from the left column and change it to a **sans serif** font by clicking on the drop-down arrow next to the Font button (see Figure 1.9), and change the font size to **26** by clicking on the drop-down arrow next to the Font Size button (see Figure 1.9). Emphasise this text by adding **bold** and **centre** alignment. Click on the bold and centre alignment buttons as shown in Figure 1.9.
2	Repeat step 1 for the text **Activities include** ensuring that the text is displayed on two lines and not hyphenated.
3	Change the remaining text to a different **serif** font with a font size of 16, **italics** and **left** aligned.
4	Add your name at the top of the left column above the clip art image.
5	Save the publication as **bears** and print one copy.

Hint:

You can change the text at step 2 by using the Format Painter icon tool. To do this highlight the text, click on **Format Painter** and select the text that is to be formatted in the same style – see Figure 1.9.

Information: Resolution and printouts

Publications can be printed in draft or at a low resolution, which saves on ink or toner. You can change the resolution of printouts, remembering that the higher the resolution the more dots there are on the page, the better quality of printout, the more ink used.

In Publisher the resolution options can be found in **Advanced Print Settings** – see Figure 1.10. To see the print options select **Print** from the **File** menu.

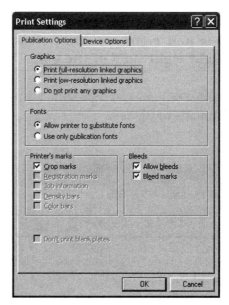

Figure 1.10 Advanced Print Settings

To produce low resolution linked graphics place a tick in the relevant box in Advanced Print options.

To change the printer to a draft resolution you may have to ask your tutor for specific instructions relating to your printer.

Task 1.7 Print resolution

Method

1   Assuming the **bears** publication is open, save the file as **bear1** and print a draft copy at a low resolution. Close the file.
Publisher can change the resolution of printing linked objects, if you click on **File**, **Print**, **Advanced Print Settings**.

2   Check the draft copy against the original and make a note of any necessary amendments.

3   Re-open the file and make any required amendments.

4   Print the publication.

5   Save and close the file.

Task 1.8 Print to file

Sometimes you might be asked to print a publication to file which can later be printed by a professional printing company. When you print to file you will be asked for a filename and a file location.

Method

1   Open the **bear1** publication and select **File** and **Print**.

2   Click in the **Print to file** box (Figure 1.11) and click **OK**.

3   Key in the filename **bears2** and click **OK**.

4   Check that the file has printed by opening your working area and where you should see the file **bears2.prn**. The file extension **.prn** indicates that this is a print file.

5   Close the file and exit Publisher.

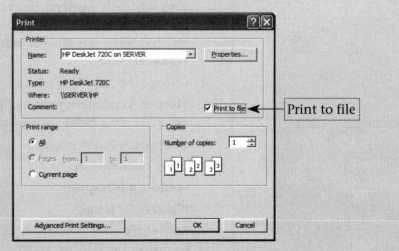

Figure 1.11 Print to file

→ Practise your skills 1

1 Create a new publication and set up a new A4 page to the following specifications:

Orientation	Landscape
Left margin	2 cm
Right margin	2 cm
Top margin	2 cm
Bottom margin	2 cm
Columns	3
Spacing	0.75 cm

2 Create a **box** border around all the three columns.

3 Key in the following text starting at the bottom of the first column:

Flower Arrangements

A new 12 week course

Designed for novices interested in flower arranging

Please contact Claire Smithson, the course leader, for further information and our enrolment details. Funding is available and some courses are free.

The course covers:

table decorations

wedding bouquets

flowers in a vase

pedestals

hand tied bouquets

and much more

You will be required to bring your own flowers and foliage for each class. One of our previous learners has started her own flower school and is offering an NVQ in Floral Design.

4 Change the following text:

Flower Arrangements and **The course covers** to **sans serif**, **18pt** size with **bold** enhancement and **centre** alignment.

5 Change the following text:

table decorations

wedding bouquets

flowers in a vase

pedestals

hand tied bouquets

and much more

to a different **serif** font, **12 pt** with **italics**.

6 Do not change the remaining text.

7 Add a suitable clip art image that spans across the top of both columns 1 and 2.

8 Save the file as **flowers** and print a draft copy at a low resolution. Close the file.

9 Check the draft copy and note any amendments.

10 Re-open the file and make the amendments.

11 Print the publication.

12 Print to file using the filename **flowers1** and click OK.

13 Close the publication and hand in to your tutor for marking.

→ Check your knowledge

1 List two different orientations of A4 paper.

2 What is the 'gutter space' on a page?

3 List two different types of border that you can add to a page.

4 Why would you print a publication at low resolution?

5 Why would you print a publication to file?

6 Why is it important to produce a draft copy of work before final printing?

7 What does RAM stand for?

8 Why should you check RAM and storage space before starting a new publication?

9 In addition to DTP software list two other programs which you may use when creating a publication.

Section 2 — Creating a master style

You will learn to

- Create a master/house style
- Set the column/gutter spacing
- Save the publication as a template
- Insert headers/footers
- Add background colour
- Insert multiple pages
- Create text styles

In this section you will create a master page which will set the margins, page orientation, text frames, gutter spacing, backgrounds, multiple pages and headers/footers. The publication will be saved as a template so that future publications can be created.

Information: Master pages

When creating publications a master page can be used and saved as a template so that it may be used for different publications or to provide consistency throughout an organisation. This means that every publication created in an organisation uses the same formatting all the time. The formatting can include text styles, background items and logos. A master page may also be known as a house style. A printing company may use a house style of 2.5 cm margins, a gutter of 1 cm, a pale blue background, with the logo in the top right corner and portrait orientation. This house style may be used for all their printing requirements, e.g. headed paper, leaflets and invoices etc. for consistency.

When creating a master page you need to think about the layout of your publication – what is its purpose, who will the reader be and what effect do you want the publication to give, so that you can plan this well in advance.

Hint:

The page margins can be seen in pink and the column guides are blue.

Task 2.1   Setting print setup

Method

1. Load Publisher, if this is not already loaded, and create a new publication.
2. Click on **File**, **Page Setup**, **Printer & Paper** and ensure that the paper size displayed is **A4 portrait**. (Click cancel to close this dialogue box.)
3. To set the margins click on **Arrange**, **Layout Guides** (see Figure 2.1) and set all margins to **3 cm** with **2 columns**.
4. Save the publication as **temp1**.

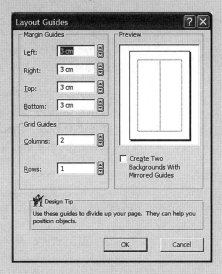

Figure 2.1 Layout Guides

Information: Column space (gutter)

The gap or spacing between columns of text can be described as the 'gutter space'. The default is 0.5 cm in Publisher. The size of the gutter can be decreased or increased depending on the amount of text to be displayed on a page. The ruler guides can help you lay out the space between columns.

Task 2.2   Setting the gutter space

Method

1. Using the publication **temp1**, draw a full size text box and click on **Format Text Box** and then select **Text Box** from the box shown in Figure 2.2.

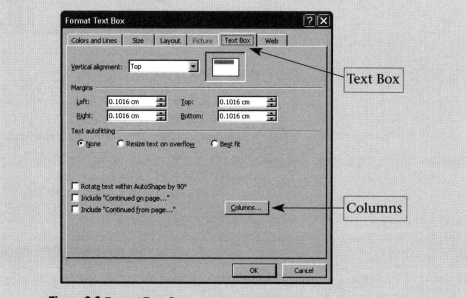

Figure 2.2 Format Text Box

2   Ensure that all the margins are displayed as **0 cm**.

3   Click on the **Columns** button (shown in Figure 2.2) and enter 2 in the **Number** space and set the **Spacing** to 0.4 cm.

4   Save the file and keep it open for the next task.

Information: Saving as a template

Once you have created a master page it should be saved as a template so that new publications can be created using the original template. Although we have only added a few items to the master page we will now save the publication as a template. Once the publication has been saved as a template you can create a new publication and save this using a different filename so that the master page remains unchanged.

Task 2.3 | Saving as a template

Method

I   Assuming the previous publication is still open save it as a template by clicking on **File**, **Save As**. The dialogue box in Figure 2.3 appears.

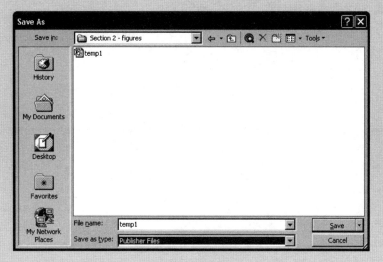

Figure 2.3 Save As

2   Enter the filename **master1** and click on the **Save as type** drop-down arrow and change the file type to show **Publisher Template** – the dialogue box in Figure 2.4 is shown.

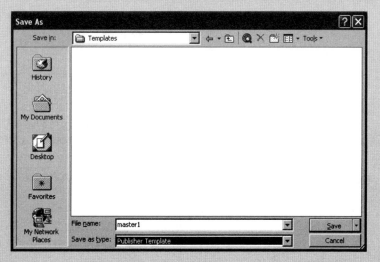

Figure 2.4 Templates folder

3 Click **Save**.

4 Close the publication.

5 To check that the publication has been saved as a template, click **File**, **New** and the Publisher catalogue is displayed, see Figure 2.5.

6 Click on **From template** and double-click on **master1** and a copy of the template is opened.

7 Keep the file open for the next task.

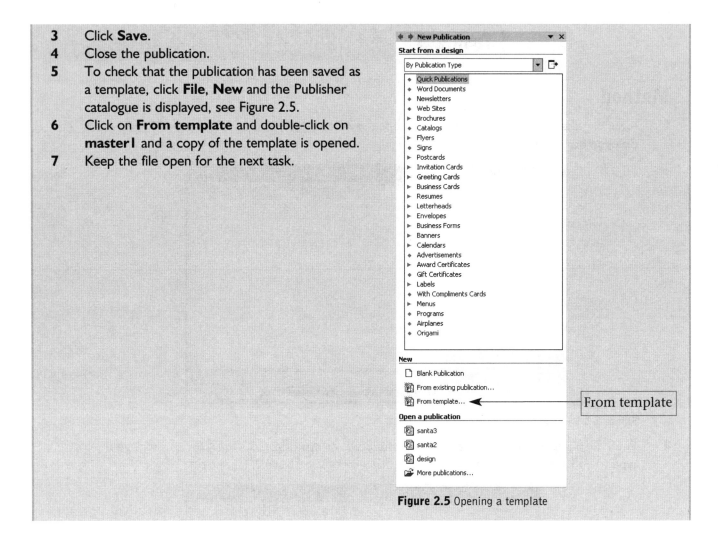

Figure 2.5 Opening a template

From template

Hint:

You can change between foreground/background using **Ctrl + M**.

Information: The Master Page

The master page in Publisher allows you to place graphics, headers and footers and page numbers on the background, and these can be repeated on every page of the publication. Items placed on the master page are viewable whilst you are working on the foreground of the publication.

Information: Running headers/footers and page numbers

Some companies use headers/footers within publications so that these items are automatically inserted into all new pages. The header/footer text can be seen above or below the main text of the publication and can include the filename of the publication, current date or details of the publication, e.g. Chapter 1. Page numbers can also be inserted easily and automatically updated. The headers/footers and page numbers are created in the master page. Running headers ensure that all copies of the header and footer are shown on all pages within the current document.

Method

1   Using the publication from Task 2.3, click on **View**, **Master Page**.
2   Draw a text box at the top of the page resting on the pink guidelines (in the header space). Click on **Format**, **Text Box**, **Size** (Figure 2.6) and ensure that the text box is set **15 cm × 1 cm**.

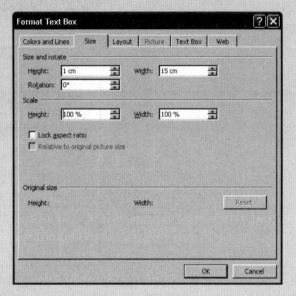

Figure 2.6 Size and Position

3   Enter the text **Master Template 1** and centre in the text box.
4   Draw a text box at the bottom of the page starting on the pink guidelines. Ensure that the text box is set to **15 cm × 1 cm**.
5   Click **Insert**, **Page Numbers**. Click **OK** to insert the page number in Current text box and show page number on first page. Publisher inserts **#**. The actual page number is displayed when you return to the foreground. Centre the page number.
6   Click on **View**, **Master Page** and ensure that the header is shown on each page and the correct page number is displayed.
7   Save the publication as a template, **template 1**, and keep the file open.

Information: Background colour

When setting a background colour you need to be aware of the cost of printing dark colours and how dark text will be displayed on a dark background. Background colour can be set as a solid colour, a pattern or as tinted shades of a full colour.

A pattern is a repeating design, for example vertical or horizontal lines. A gradient uses tints or shades of one colour to create a special pattern of increasing shades.

Task 2.5   Setting a background colour

Method

1   Using the **template 1** template select the text box, click on **Format**, **Text Box**, click on the drop down arrow under **Fill Color:** and choose **More Colors**.

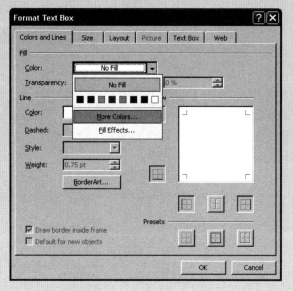

Figure 2.7 Colour formatting

2   Now select a **pale blue** colour from the palette (Figure 2.8).

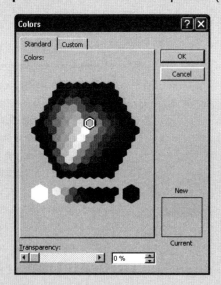

Figure 2.8 Colours

3   Click **OK** twice – the background colour will be applied to the text box.

4   To change the background texture click on **Format**, **Text Box**, **Fill Color**, **Fill Effects**, **Pattern** (see Figure 2.9 below).

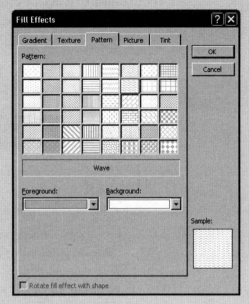

Figure 2.9 Pattern

5   Select one of the patterns displayed and ensure that the **Foreground** is showing blue and **Background** is white.

6   Click **OK** twice.

7   Save the file as a template as **master2**.

Hint:

Instead of applying a base colour or pattern effect to the background a gradient fill can be applied. A gradient is a gradual blend between two or more colours.

Information: Layers

When filling text frames/images you may have to work with layers where one layer of text can be placed on another layer, for example a filled text box. By selecting one layer you can either **Bring it to the front** 🗗 or **Send it to the back** 🗗 allowing you to see both layers.

Try it out

Create a new publication and try adding different colours and patterns. Add text in different colours and try and find one which you find appealing and easy to read.

Information: Adding borders

The following is the method for adding borders.

1   Using the publication template **master2** add a border around both columns as a **box** with **1pt** thickness.

2   Click on **Format**, **Text Box Line Color**: and select black line as a grid with 1pt weight.

Remember:

To add a text box, click on the text box tool.

> **Information:** Multiple pages
>
> In Publisher you can insert new pages which are blank, which have a text frame on each page, or all items you have previously set in which (e.g. text frames, background etc.) can be duplicated on the inserted pages.

Task 2.6 | Inserting multiple pages

Method

1 Using the template **master2** add three additional pages to create a four-page publication.

2 Click on **Insert Page** and the dialogue box in Figure 2.10 is shown.

3 Enter the number **3** into the **Number of new pages** box and click on **Duplicate all objects on page** to allow all formatting that has been set to be created on the new pages.

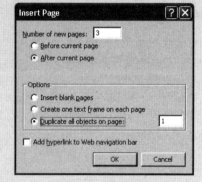

Figure 2.10 Insert Page

4 Click **OK**. At the bottom of the screen you will now see **4 pages** (see Figure 2.11).

Figure 2.11 Inserted pages

5 Save the **master2** publication as a template and close the file.

→ Practise your skills 1

1 Create a new master template – **A4 landscape**, margins of **4 cm**.

2 Draw a text box with **3** columns and a gutter of **0.7 cm**. Add a grid border with a **4pt** line style.

3 Draw a text box and add pale purple background fill with a checkered fill effect using both Base color and Color 2 as pale burgundy.

4 Draw a header text box in the background **21.7 cm × 1 cm** and enter the text, left aligned:

→

Fleur Today

5 Draw a footer text box in the background **21.7 cm** × **1 cm** and enter a page number (centred) and your name and date (right aligned).

6 Insert a suitable logo onto the background in the top right corner (header space) of the page using a clip art image.

7 Save the publication as a template using the filename **master3**.

8 Produce a screen printout to show that the publication has been correctly saved as a template.

→ Practise your skills 2

1 Create a new master template – **A4 portrait**, margins of **2 cm**.

2 Draw a text box with **2** columns and a gutter of **0.5 cm**. Add a grid border with a **1pt** line style.

3 Add a pale yellow background fill with a brick effect pattern.

4 Draw a header text box in the background **17 cm** × **0.7 cm** and enter the text:

New Carz

5 Draw a footer text box in the background **17 cm** × **0.7 cm** and enter a page number (centred) and your name and date (right aligned).

6 Save the publication as a template using the filename **master4**.

7 Produce a screen printout to show that the publication has been correctly saved as a template. Keep the template open.

Information: Text styles

By selecting margins, type style and size of text, alignment and line length for the page you can create a master page/style sheet for the publication using different styles for the heading, subheadings and body text. All the text formatting which is consistent throughout an organisation can be called the 'house style'. Subheadings can also be described as 'side-headings'.

Method

1   Create a new publication based on the **master1** template, click **Format, Styles and Formatting** and the task pane in Figure 2.12 is shown.

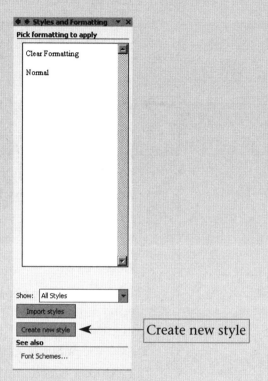

Figure 2.12 Text Style

2   Click on **Create New Style** and enter new style name **Heading** (Figure 2.13).

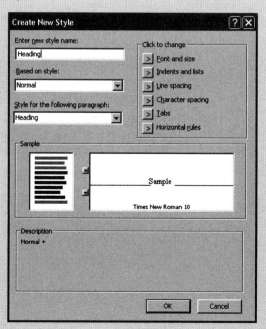

Figure 2.13 Create New Style

3	Click on **Font and size** and change the font to **Arial** and size to **36 pt** and tick **All Caps** and click **OK**.
4	Click on **Indents and Lists** and change the alignment to **centre** and click **OK**.
5	Click **OK** again.
6	Repeat steps 2 and 3 and create a subheading style – enter new style name: **Subhead**.
7	Change the font to **Times New Roman** and size **20 pt**.
8	Repeat steps 2 and 3 and create a new body style – enter new style name: **body**.
9	Change the font to **Comic Sans Ms**, size **14 pt** and **justified**.
10	Click **OK** and close the **Text Style** box.
11	Save the publication as **master5** as a template.

Information: Alignment of text

Text can be aligned to the left margin, right margin, centred or justified. House styles usually include the alignment of text (see page 9 for examples of alignment).

Task 2.8   Alignment of text

Method

1	Using the master template **master5** change the subhead text style to right alignment. (Remember: **Format**, **Styles and Formatting**, **Subhead**, **Modify**.)
2	Change the heading to be left aligned.
3	Amend the body text to be centre aligned.
4	Save the publication as **master5** and close the file.

Information: Custom page sizes

At times you may wish to create a publication which is different from A4 but will still be printed onto A4 paper. For this you can create a custom page. Custom pages can also be produced as folded booklets and leaflets. By accessing the **File**, **Page Setup** menu you can choose a publication type from the layout tab. To check custom size printouts, crop marks can be printed to show the size of the paper size created. These are covered in Section 12.

Method

1   Create a new publication with the page size **19 cm × 25 cm** with **portrait** orientation. Set the margins to be **2 cm** all round. From **Layout tab** select **Folded Card** from the **Publication type** list.
2   Create a text box to fill the page and key in the text **Custom Page**.
3   Change the colour of the text to be yellow with bold effect.
4   Produce a screen print of the Custom Page dialogue box showing the page setup you have created and show it to your tutor.

→ Practise your skills 3

1   Create a new greeting card publication by selecting the **Folded Card** option from the Publication layout with **portrait** orientation. Retain the default sizes by clicking **OK**, and add a text box for the header. Click **Yes** to the prompt that appears.
2   Change the margins to **1 cm** all round.
3   Add the header **greeting1** right aligned.
4   Draw a text box and add a suitable background colour.
5   Create two new text styles – one for the heading and one for the body text. Use two different sans serif fonts. Set two different font sizes. Use appropriate alignment.
6   Insert the following text:
   Congratulations
   A new job!
   Good luck with your promotion
7   Apply a suitable border.
8   Save the publication as **practice1**, print one copy of the file and hand it to your tutor for marking. Close the file.

→ Practise your skills 4

1   Create a new publication by creating a custom size publication of **18 cm x 24 cm – portrait** orientation.
2   Change the margins to **1 cm** all round and change the display to two columns with a column space of **0.3 cm**.
3   Add a text frame.
4   Add the header **custom** left aligned and add a page number right aligned.
5   Add a suitable background colour as a tinted colour.

6   Create two new text styles – one for the heading and one for the body text. Use two different serif fonts. Set two different font sizes. Use appropriate alignment.

7   Insert the following text (Remember to apply appropriate text styles and sizes.):

The Data Protection Act

The Data Protection Act of 1998 was created and identified eight principles of which data could be held.

The principles state that data must be:

1. **fairly and lawfully processed;**
2. **processed for limited purposes;**
3. **adequate, relevant and not excessive;**
4. **accurate;**
5. **not kept for longer than is necessary;**
6. **processed in line with your rights;**
7. **secure; and,**
8. **not transferred to countries without adequate protection.**

By law data controllers have to keep to these principles.

The Information Commissioner and his staff ensure that organisations that are processing data are doing so in line with the obligations that are placed upon them by the various pieces of legislation such as: the Data Protection Act, Freedom of Information Act and the Privacy and Electronic Communications Regulations.

This Act places obligations on data users to:

register data held and usage with the Data Protection Commission;

hold data for only the purpose that it has been registered.

As an individual you can ask for a copy of any information held on you by an organisation. This is commonly known as "Subject Access Request".

Further information can be found on the Information Commission's official website.

8   Insert a suitable clip art image in the lower right-hand corner of the publication.

9   Apply a suitable border.

10 Save the publication as **practice2** as a template. Print one copy.

→ Check your knowledge

1   What is the purpose and role of a house style?

2   Why would you use a master page?

3   Why would you save a publication as a template?

4   What three things should you consider when using colour?

5   What is the background of a publication?

Section 3 | Working with text

You will learn to

- Create .rtf files
- Create .txt files
- Create .doc files

In this section you will learn to produce text that can be imported into different publications and how to create different kinds of files.

Information: Text

Text can be saved in different file formats to enable users to open/edit files before importing them into a publication. Text saved in different file formats allows users using different software or using different languages to open the files and insert the text.

Files are saved in standard text formats, for example:

- **.rtf** stands for rich text format and means that all formatting instructions are saved which can then be converted into a compatible word processing document.
- **.txt** stands for plain text format and means that only the plain text is saved and all formatting instructions are lost.
- **.doc** is the standard file format using Microsoft Word.

In this section you will use a text editor (e.g. notepad or wordpad) and a word processor to create, edit and save a text file which can be imported into a publication later in the book.

Task 3.1 | Create a text file

Method

1 Open **Microsoft Notepad**. You can find notepad by clicking on the **Start** button, **Programs**, **Accessories** and **Notepad**. Text files created in notepad will be created using plain text without any formatting.

2 Key in the following text:

Bags to Love
Our new company has developed a new product which allows you to turn a special photograph into a special gift.
Imagine having that special photograph made into a unique handbag, notebook or diary which can be cherished for years to come.

3 Save the file as **bags** as a **.txt** file in your working area and close the file.

Task 3.2 — Open a text file

Method

1. Assuming **Notepad** is still open – open the file **bags**.
2. Print one copy of the file.
3. Close the file.

Task 3.3 — Amend a text file

Method

1. Assuming **Notepad** is still open – open the file **bags**.
2. Amend the text file by keying in the following text as the last two paragraphs:
   For further details, please contact us on 08090 7647581.
   Prices start from £49.50.
3. Save the file as **bags1** as a text file, print one copy and close the file and exit from Notepad.

Try it out

Find some suitable text that you wish to display in a poster or newspaper article and key this directly into a word processing document. Save the text as a suitable filename ready to be imported into Publisher.

→ Practise your skills 1

1. Open **Microsoft Notepad**.
2. Key in the following text:

   Special Gifts

   Looking for that unusual gift? Why not consider drama tokens?

   Drama tokens are welcomed at over 210 theatres nationwide including those in the West End allowing you to choose what you want to see, when and where.

   You can choose from classical ballet, comedy, dramas and blockbuster musicals.

3. Save the file as **theatre** as a text file, print and close the file.

4 Open the file **theatre** in a text editor and make the following changes:

- Change the word **drama** at the end of the first line to **theatre** and the first word at the beginning of the second paragraph.
- Add the following text as the last paragraph:
  Theatre tokens are available in £1, £5, £10 and £20 denominations and have no expiry date.

5 Save the file as **theatre1** as a text file and print this file.

→ Practise your skills 2

1 Open **Microsoft Notepad**.

2 Key in the following text:

Speciality Parties!

We are pleased to announce a new service for those of you who love parties!

We can organise a themed party of your choice on your behalf:

Elvis Moments

The best of the 60s

Walt Disney

Furry Friends

And many more

3 Save the file as **party** as a text file, print and close the file.

4 Open the file **party** in a text editor and make the following changes.

Add the following text as the last paragraph:

We can select the venue and take care of everything including the cleaning up! Select one from the range above or tell us your theme and we will see if we can accommodate your requirements!

5 Save the file as **party1** as a text file, print and close this file.

→ Practise your skills 3

1 Open **Microsoft Word**.

2 Key in the following text:

Christmas Fayre

All Saints' Christmas Fayre

Saturday 13 December

Come and meet Santa Claus in the Church Hall

3 Save the file as **Santa** as a rich text file (.rtf). To do this you will need to click on **File**, **Save As** and change the **Save as type** to .rtf.

4 Print and close the file.

5 Open the file **Santa** in a text editor and make the following changes.

Add the following text as the last paragraph:

Stalls include:

Christmas Crafts

Tombola

Decoupage

Refreshments

Games

6 Save the file as **santa1** in the same format and print one copy.

7 Close the file.

→ Check your knowledge

1 What do the following file extensions mean?

(a) .rtf

(b) .txt

(c) .doc

2 Describe why you would create a text style.

Section 4 | Text layouts

You will learn to

- Apply bulleted and numbered lists
- Apply indents/hanging indents
- Apply rotated/skewed text
- Apply banner headlines
- Apply callout boxes

Information: Text layout

Text layouts enhance the text that is displayed on the page and in this section we will look at how different effects can be achieved using different text layouts.

Information: Bulleted and numbered lists

Bulleted and numbered lists can enhance and emphasise certain words in the text.

Task 4.1 | Bullets and numbering

Method

1   Create a new publication with **A4 portrait** orientation, **2 cm** margins all round.

2   Create a text box around this area and key in the following text:

The organisation is to introduce an absence management policy which staff will be expected to follow from the new year. This policy has been introduced because different departments/sections within the organisation were operating their own procedures which were not consistent throughout the organisation.

The policy will address:
Staff with frequent short term absences
Staff who are on long term absence
Lateness
Compassionate leave
Unpaid leave

It is hoped that this policy will provide a consistent approach to employees within the organisation and enable Managers to maintain accurate records of absence which are now required by our auditors.

3 Highlight the text **Staff with frequent . . . to unpaid leave** and apply bullets to this text. To do this click on **Format, Indents and Lists** (Figure 4.1).

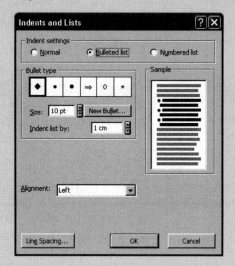

Figure 4.1 Indents and Lists

4 Select **Bulleted list** from the **Indent settings** options and select the diamond icon.

5 Click **OK**.

6 Save the publication as **absence**, print one copy and close the file.

Try it out

Using the **absence** publication change the bulleted text and apply different numbered/bulleted icons to the text. Go back into the **Format** menu and **Indents and Lists**, click **Bulleted list** and change the character to the one you want. Click **OK**.

To change to a numerical list click on **Numbered list** instead of **Bulleted list** in the **Indents and Lists** sub-menu.

Information: Indents and hanging indents

Indents and hanging indents can assist you in placing items on the page and displaying text and white space effectively. Indents are usually between both left and right margins.

Here is an example of indents:

> **This text has been keyed in and indented 2 cm from the left margin only.**

This text has been keyed in to show how text can be indented 2 cm from the right margin only.

> **This text has been keyed in as an example showing how text can be indented from both the left and right margins by 2 cm.**

This text has been keyed in as an example of how text can be shown as a hanging indent at 2 cm.

Method

I	Open the publication **absence** and highlight the bulleted text. To indent this paragraph by 2.5 cm, click **Format, Indents and Lists** (see Figure 4.1). Change **Indent list by:** to 2 cm.
2	This text will now be indented.
3	Save the publication and close the file.

Try it out

1   Open the publication **practice2**.
2   Highlight the text beginning **Register data** and ending **subject on request**. This paragraph will be indented with a hanging indent **2 cm** at both left and right margins.
3   Save the file as **try1** and close the publication.

Information: Rotated/skewed text

In Publisher it is easy to rotate or skew any text or images. This can change the effect of how text appears on the page. For example, you can rotate the title of a document so that it appears down the left-hand side of the page instead of at the top of the page. Text can be rotated by a precise angle or by 5° using the Rotate dialogue box. Objects can be rotated manually by holding down one of the objects' handles.

An example of how to rotate – remember a full rotation is 360°.

For this rotation	Type
↓	0°
←	90°
↑	180°
→	270°

Method

1. Create a new publication based on the template **master2**. Create a text box in the left-hand column and insert the text from the text file **Santa** by choosing **Text file** from the **Insert** menu.
2. Delete pages 2, 3 and 4 as these will not be used in this publication.
3. Insert the text file **santa1** and apply a border to this box.
4. Rotate this text 65°. Select the text box and click on **Format Text Box, Size, Rotation**.
   The dialogue box in Figure 4.2 is shown. Key 65 in the **Rotation** box.
5. Save the publication as **santa2** and print one copy.
6. Close the file.

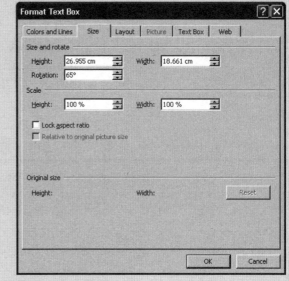

Figure 4.2 Rotating text

Information: Banner headlines

A headline as a banner can be an object of text in its own text box which is separate from the main body text of the document. In Publisher you can use WordArt, which can help produce professional, colourful banner headlines with ease.

Method

1. Open the publication **santa2** and create a banner headline.
2. Create a new **WordArt Frame** by clicking on the **Insert WordArt** tool.
3. Key in the text:
   BRING YOUR FAMILY AND FRIENDS
   Select **Arch Up (Curve)** from Figure 4.3.
4. Move the WordArt frame to the top of the page and resize so that it fits within the pink guidelines.

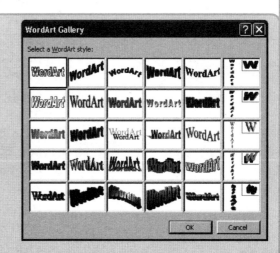

Figure 4.3 WordArt Gallery

5   Increase the size of the body text and use an appropriate font style to display on this poster.

6   Save the file as **santa3** and print one copy of your publication.

7   Close the file.

Information: Text density

Text density is sometimes referred to in desktop publishing and simply means the thickness of the print. Bold is one way to make the text thicker and darker and therefore more prominent.

Information: Callout boxes

Callout boxes add interest to text and attract the reader's attention to certain words. You need to consider formatting of the text, for example bold, larger font, shading and borders, to add more emphasis.

Task 4.5   Callout boxes

Method

I   Create a new publication based on the **master3** template, and create a new text box and key in the following text:

City Life!

Visit London Today and discover:

Museums of History

Art

Science and Technology

Castles, Palaces and Historic Buildings

The City of London is a thriving, busy city famous for its landmarks, the Old Bailey and the financial heart of the UK.

There are hundreds of places of interest to visit, including the home of our Royal Family, Buckingham Palace.

The Palace is open for a short time each year and you can visit parts of it that the Queen and her family have made available to the public.

Inside you will see fabulous treasures of the British monarchy. The Palace employs its own tour guides, who are always on hand to help you with any queries you may have and provide any information you need on the priceless collections of paintings, porcelain, furniture and antiques.

Once you have been inside the Palace you can wander around the gardens and the lake and forget you are in the middle of a bustling city centre!

Visit London Today!

2 Create a new text box between the lines of text **Castles, Palaces...** and **Visit our ... details** and add the text:
We offer a special discount to school parties and youth groups during the summer term.

3 Change the text in this box to **Cooper Black** font with a font size of **14 pt**.

4 Change the header text to display **London**.

5 Add a **border** using **black dots** from the **Border Art** selection in the Format Text Box options and shade the box to **pale pink**.

6 Place an image in the top right-hand corner of column 3.

7 Place the text box in the bottom right-hand part of column 3.

8 Save the publication as **London**, print one copy and close the file.

→ Practise your skills 1

1 Create a new publication based on the **master4** template.

2 Create a banner headline **LUXURY CRUISES** using WordArt and the **Wave1** style.

3 Rotate this heading **90°** and align this down the left-hand side of the page.

4 Key in the following text in column 2:

Hawaii Express

Nights of luxurious pampering aboard the Hawaii Express Cruise Liner leaving Gatwick on the first Friday of each month. Return flights to your own local airport included.

The Cruise Liner visits:

Honolulu

Nawiliwili

Lahaina

Kona

5 Use appropriate font style and size to fill half of the space in this column.

6 Change the header text to display **Hawaii**.

7 Add suitable bullets to the last four items starting with **Honolulu** and ending with **Kona**.

8 Create a new text box at the bottom of the page and add the following text:

Special Offers

Between

January and March

9 Use appropriate font style and size to fill this text area.

10 Rotate this text box **55°**.

11 Add a border and background colour to this box to emphasise the text as a callout box.

12 Save the publication as **Hawaii** and print one copy of your publication.

→ Practise your skills 2

1 Create a new publication based on the **master3** template.

2 Create a banner headline **A NEW CAR** using WordArt.

3 Rotate this heading **270°** and align this down the right-hand side of the page.

4 Key in the following text starting at the top of the first column:

Looking for a new car?

Why not visit our new auto-parc?

A new way of shopping for a new car – instead of visiting separate garages to get that best price why not visit the auto-parc which comprises 40 individual garages all on one site.

We can offer you:

Finance

A great deal

An excellent coffee house

Hundreds of new and used cars to choose from.

5 Use appropriate font style and size to fill this space.

6 Change the header text to display **Cars**.

7 Add suitable bullets to the last four items starting with **Finance** and ending with **choose from**.

8 Create a new text box at the top of the second column and add the following text:

Open seven days per week until 8 pm each evening!

9 Use appropriate font style and size to fill this text area.

10 Rotate this text box **285°**.

11 Add a border and background colour to this box to emphasise the text as a callout box.

12 Save the publication as **Cars** and print one copy of your publication.

→ Check your knowledge

1 When would you use a callout box?

2 What is meant by 'rotated text'?

3 What is the purpose of applying 'text density' when creating a publication?

4 What is a banner headline?

5 Why would you create a .txt file and import this into a publication rather than creating the text directly into the publication?

Section 5

Text enhancements and formats

You will learn to

- Apply bold, italics, roman, uppercase
- Apply underline
- Apply dropped and raised caps
- Apply reverse text
- Apply strikethrough
- Apply subscript/superscript

Information: Bold, italics, roman, underline

Text can be enhanced using some of the functions listed below:

Text enhancement	Example
Bold	**Bold** text
Italics	*Italics* text
Roman	Plain text
Underline	<u>Underline</u>
Uppercase	UPPERCASE

Further information on the text enhancements can be found on page 9.

Task 5.1 — Enhancing text

Method

1   Open the publication **absence** and make the following text enhancements:
    Embolden the words **The policy will address.**
    Underline the words **Managers to maintain accurate records** from the last paragraph.
    Italicise all the bulleted text.
    Increase the size of the font for the whole publication.
2   Save a copy of the publication as **enhance** and close the file.

Task 5.2	Drop cap

Method

1. Create a new **A4 portrait** publication with **2 cm** margins all round.
2. Add a banner headline at the top **The Cook Islands**.
3. Add the following text using a **16pt** size:

   The islands were named after Captain James Cook when he became the first European to see them. The main island, known as Rarotonga, became a British protectorate in 1888, and in 1901 became part of New Zealand, and was discovered by the Bounty Mutineers in 1789.

   The best swimming beaches are at Muri Lagoon and Titikaveka. There is an excellent museum at Takamoa and a village tour allows you to see the locals demonstrating their weaving, coconut husking and carving.

   The currency is the New Zealand dollar and there are plenty of currency exchanges available on the islands.

4. Add a drop capital to the **T** of the word **The** for each of the three paragraphs. Click **Format**, **Drop Cap** and the dialogue box in Figure 5.1 is shown.

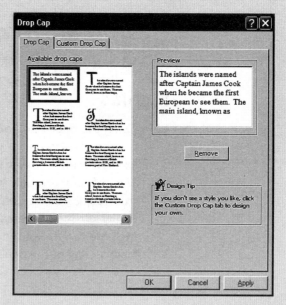

Figure 5.1 Drop Cap

5   Click the first example from the second row, click **Apply** and click **OK** to close the dialogue box.

6   Check your publication for errors and make any necessary amendments.

7   Save the publication as **cook**, print one copy of the file and close the file.

Note: Publisher has default Drop Cap formats or allows you to create your own custom drop cap. To do this click **Format**, **Drop Cap**, and click **Custom Drop Cap** – when this dialogue box opens (see Figure 5.2) you can change the **Size of letters**, e.g. three lines deep, by increasing or decreasing this number. For the purpose of this qualification the **Number of letters** will remain at 1.

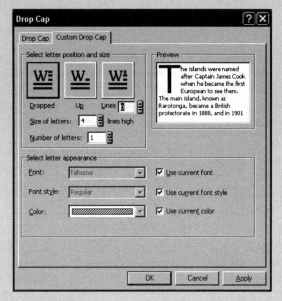

Figure 5.2 Custom Drop Cap

Information: Reverse text

Reverse text can be used when you want to use white text on a black or coloured background.

Task 5.3	**Reverse text**

Method

1   Create a new publication **A4 portrait** with **3cm** margins all round.

2   Create a text frame and key in the following text using an **18 pt** size:
Estonia is bordered by the Baltic Sea and the Russian Federation and Latvia and is a country of great scenic beauty with many forests, lakes and islands.

3   Fill the text box with a black fill by clicking on the **Fill Color** icon.

4   Highlight the text in the text box and change this to white by clicking on the **Font Color** icon.

5   Save the publication with the filename **Estonia** and print one copy and close the file.

Information: Strikethrough

The strikethrough formatting allows you to show words that have been crossed out.

Try it out

Using a different desktop publishing package find a strikethrough formatting option and key in your name and date to see the effect.

Information: Subscript and superscript

Subscript or superscript text can be applied to the text that is produced just above or below the normal line of text, for example a footnote reference. Other examples include:

Text enhancement	Example
Superscript	$^{\circ}C$ 4th March
Subscript	H_2O

Hint:

You can use keyboard shortcuts to apply subscripts and superscripts. To apply or remove subscript formatting click on the keyboard shortcut:

Ctrl+=

To apply or remove superscript formatting click on the keyboard shortcut shown:

Ctrl+Shift+=

Task 5.4 — Applying subscript and superscript

Method

1 Create a new publication with **A4 landscape** orientation and draw a text box.
2 Add the following text:
   H20 are launching their new aqua range of swimwear on the 22nd June.
   Further details will be available soon.
3 Apply a subscript to the **2** in **H20** and a superscript to **nd** in **22nd June**.
4 To do this, highlight the appropriate text, click **Format, Font** (Figure 5.3) and place a tick in the appropriate Effects box.
5 Close the file without saving any changes.

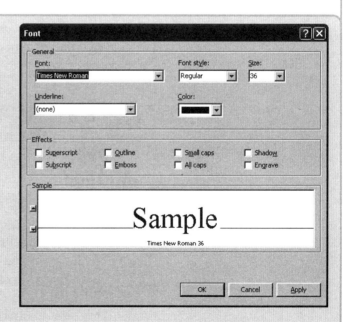

Figure 5.3 Font

→ Practise your skills 1

1 Create a new publication with **A4 portrait** orientation with **2 cm** margins all round.

2 Key in the following text using a **16 pt** size:

Internet Banking

Online or Internet banking offers you the main banking services with the ability to manage your investments and mortgages online.

Internet banking allows you to view balances and statements, you can transfer funds between accounts, pay bills and set up standing orders. If you have additional products such as credit cards, you can also check and repay outstanding balances. One organisation allows you to add all your accounts to your portfolio which can all be viewed simultaneously once you have logged onto a secure area.

Some Internet banking facilities were set up just to allow customers to bank online, however, many high street traditional banks now offer their customers this service allowing them to manage their finances without visiting the branch.

Updated 1st January

3 Choose a suitable emphasis to enhance the following words:

Internet Banking

4 Apply a drop cap to the first letter of each paragraph.

5 Apply a superscript to **st** of **1st**.

6 Apply a background fill to the text frame.

7 Reverse the text in the text frame to be white on black.

8 Add in today's date and your name as a footer.

9 Save the publication as **banking**.

10 Close and print one copy of the file using low printing resolution.

11 Proofread the publication carefully, make any amendments and print one final copy of the publication. Remember that you can use the spellcheck to identify any spelling errors but you should proofread very carefully.

12 Ensure that you have saved the publication and closed the file.

→ Practise your skills 2

1 Create a new publication with **A4 portrait** orientation with **2 cm** margins all round.

2 Key in the following text in **14 pt** size:

What is Interior Design?

Our Special Interior Design service specialises in the following areas and provides the following services:

Elements of design include colour, shape, texture and noise and therefore our designer will see how you respond to these elements in order to provide you with the best designed space that you can live in for years to come!

Our designers have access to the latest fashion of furniture, fabrics, accessories and ornaments and will be able to show you examples of products that are available. Our catalogue covers the minimalist, the traditional, the Victorian era and 21st century designs.

Our designer will provide you with the plans within 48 hours of the first consultation!

3 Apply a raise cap to the first of the two paragraphs of text only.

4 Create another text box in between '**Our Special Interior Design . . .** ' and '**Elements . . .** ' and key in the following text:

- **Assessing the way the space will be used**
- **Calculating the dimensions of the space**
- **Identifying the significance of the space**
- **Considering, for example, light acoustics or any special needs or disabilities to be catered for.**

5 Emphasise the following words using either bold, italics or underline:

All the bulleted text

6 Apply a background fill to this text frame only.

7 Reverse the text in this text frame only so that the text is white on a black background and is visible.

8 Change the text 21st to be a superscript.

9 Add your name as a header.

10 Add border effects to the two different text boxes.

11 Save the publication as **design**.

12 Close and print one copy of the file using low printing resolution.

13 Proofread the publication carefully, make any amendments and print one final copy of the publication.

14 Ensure that you have saved the publication and closed the file.

→ Check your knowledge

1 What is meant by the following text enhancements?

    (a) Bold

    (b) Italics

    (c) Roman

    (d) Underline

2 Why would you insert a drop cap?

3 What is a raised cap?

4 What is meant by strikethrough?

5 What is the difference between subscript and superscript?

Section 6 | Working with folders

You will learn to

- Create and open folders
- Move files between folders
- Delete a publication/file
- Save into a folder
- Save to floppy disk

It's important that you know how to manage your files and folders so that you are able to locate files quickly on the computer, just the same as being able to locate paper copies in a filing cabinet.

You will need a formatted floppy disk for some tasks in this section.

Information: Folders

At Level 1 you learnt how to manage files and folders. The first revision tasks asked you to save files in your working folder and this may have been **My Documents** or **My Work**. On a single computer that is not linked via a network, files will usually be saved onto the **c:\ drive**. If you are working at college you will probably be on a network and your supervisor will be able to tell you which drive you should be saving work to.

Files should be organised into categories by creating folders and putting related files together. Folders and files should be given relevant names. A sub-folder is a folder within a folder, for example you create a new folder named Desktop Publishing but within this folder you want a separate sub-folder named Images and one called Publications. This allows you to file your work more effectively.

Close any programs that you have open and return to the Windows desktop. The icon opposite shows My Documents which will probably be similar to the one that you are able to see depending on the software version you are using. Double-click on this icon and the My Documents folder will open.

Task 6.1   Create folders

Method

1   Click **File**, **New**. A side menu appears (Figure 6.1).
2   Click on **Folder**.
3   A new folder appears and the name **New Folder** is highlighted.
4   Key in the name **tasks**.
5   Press **Enter**.
6   Repeat the process and create a new folder named **practice** as a sub-folder of **My Documents**.

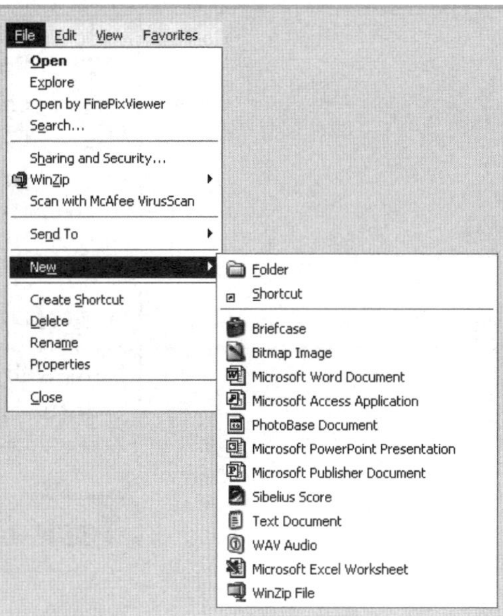

File	Edit	View	Favorites

Open
Explore
Open by FinePixViewer
Search...

Sharing and Security...
WinZip ▸
Scan with McAfee VirusScan

Send To ▸

New ▸

Create Shortcut
Delete
Rename
Properties

Close

▸
📁 Folder
▫ Shortcut

📦 Briefcase
🖼 Bitmap Image
📘 Microsoft Word Document
📄 Microsoft Access Application
📄 PhotoBase Document
📊 Microsoft PowerPoint Presentation
📄 Microsoft Publisher Document
📄 Sibelius Score
📄 Text Document
🎵 WAV Audio
📗 Microsoft Excel Worksheet
📦 WinZip File

Figure 6.1 Creating a new folder

Task 6.2   Open folders

Method

1   Double-click on the **My Documents** icon on the desktop.
2   Click on the **Folders** icon on the Standard toolbar.
3   You will now be able to see the **My Documents** folder and the two new sub-folders **tasks** and **practice** below.

Task 6.3   Move files between folders

Method

1   Locate the **bears2** file from within your working folder and holding the left mouse button down, drag the file into the **practice** folder and release. The file has now been moved.
2   Locate the **flowers** and **revise1** files from within your working folder and move the files into the **tasks** folder.

Task 6.4	Delete a file

Method

1 Search for the text file **Santa** and select it.
2 Press the delete key on the keyboard. You will be prompted to confirm the delete. Click **Yes**.
3 Close the folder window by clicking the **Close** icon ☒ in the top right corner of the window.

Information: Reorganising files

As well as reorganising files into folders, you can save them directly into folders when you create them.

Task 6.5	Copy a file

Method

1 Locate the **flowers** file from within your **tasks** folder.
2 Copy the **flowers** file by clicking on the copy icon and pasting the file into the **practice** folder.
3 Produce a screen print showing the contents of the **tasks** and **practice** folders.

Task 6.6	Save a publication into a folder

Method

1 Load Publisher and create a new blank publication.
2 Create a text box and key in the following text:

City and Guilds Equals – Desktop Publishing Level 2

3 Click on the **File** menu and choose **Save**. The **Save As** dialogue box appears (Figure 6.2).

Figure 6.2 Save As

4   Double-click on the **tasks** folder. The **Save in** box now shows that the **tasks** folder is open (Figure 6.3).

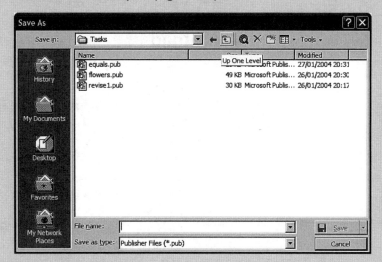

Figure 6.3 Save in box

5   Key in the filename **equals**, and click on **Save**.

6   Close the publication.

Task 6.7	Save to another folder

Method

1   Create a new publication and create a text box. Key in the following text:

   Daffodils usually begin to flower in March

2   Click on the **File** menu and select **Save**. The **Save As** dialogue box opens as in Figure 6.2.

3   The **Save in** box still reads **tasks** as this was the folder you had last used.

4   Click on the **Up One Level** icon ⬆ and the **Save in** box now reads **My Documents**.

5   Double-click the **practice** folder. The **Save in** box should now read **practice**.

6   Key in a suitable name, e.g. **daffodils**.

7   Click on **Save**.

Information: Saving to floppy disk

You may wish to save files to floppy disk or as a backup copy in case the original file becomes damaged or you want to work on the file elsewhere.

Task 6.8 | Save a file to a floppy disk

Method

1. Insert a floppy disk into the disk drive with the label uppermost and nearest to you.
2. Using the file **daffodils**, select **Save As** from the **File** menu.
3. Click on the drop-down arrow after the **Save in** practice folder and select the $3\frac{1}{2}$ **Floppy (A:)**.
4. Key in the filename **daffodils** and click on **Save**.
5. Close the publication.
6. Once the disk drive light has gone off remove the floppy disk from the drive.
7. You now have a copy of the **daffodils** folder on floppy disk and also in the **practice** folder.

→ Practise your skills 1

1. Create a new folder called **management**.
2. Move the files **absence** and **cars** from your working area into this folder.
3. Produce a screen printout of the folder **management**.

→ Practise your skills 2

1. Create a new folder called **hols**.
2. Copy the files **cook** and **Estonia** from your working area into this folder.
3. Produce a screen printout of the folder **hols**.

→ Practise your skills 3

1. Open your working area and delete the file **revise1**.
2. Open the folder **practice** and delete the file **daffodils**.
3. Produce a screen printout to show the contents of the **practice** folder.

→ Practise your skills 4

1. Create a new folder **master** onto a floppy disk.
2. Move the file **London**.
3. Copy the file **Hawaii**.
4. Create a sub-folder called **backup** of the folder **master**.

→ Check your knowledge

1. Why is it good practice to create different folders for files?
2. What is the difference between moving and copying a file?

Consolidation 1

1 Create a new directory/folder named **consolidation**.

2 Create a new master template – A4 portrait, margins of 2 cm.

3 Draw a text frame with 2 columns and a gutter of 0.5 cm. Add a grid border with a 1pt line style.

4 Add a pale pink background fill with a line effect pattern.

5 Draw a header text box in the background 17 cm × 0.7 cm and enter the text:

Change Management

6 Draw a footer text box in the background 17 cm × 0.7 cm and enter a page number (centred) and your name and date (right aligned).

7 Save the publication as a template using the **master5** template. Keep the template open.

8 Create a new publication based on the **master5** template.

9 Create a banner headline **CHANGE FATIGUE** using WordArt.

10 Key in the following text starting at the top of the first column:

Too much change, too fast, too often!

Change fatigue can be caused by rapid change which has been poorly managed.

The change can cause uncertainty, demotivation and stress so individuals become demoralised.

Individual and team performance drops and absenteeism increases.

The fatigue results when the drivers for change, eg technology, new regulations or rulings, are uncoordinated and companies try to re-engineer themselves as quickly as possible in order to respond to customer needs but to drive costs down wherever possible.

Avoid Change Fatigue

- **Evaluate and revisit corporate plans to make sure you are still on track**
- **Don't destroy old systems until the new ones are fully installed and staff are trained.**

11 Create a new text box at the end of the text and key in the following text:

Remember your body needs to recover!

12 Rotate this text box to the right and align this down the right-hand side of the page.

13 Use appropriate font style and size to fill this space.

14 Add suitable bullets to the last two items starting, **Evaluate and revisit ...**

15 Insert a suitable clip art image in the lower right corner.

16 Save the publication as **fatigue** in the **consolidation** directory/folder and print one copy of your publication.

You will learn to

- Create simple graphics using a graphics editor
- Scan images into a graphics editor
- Scan images directly into Publisher
- Capture images into a graphics editor
- Capture images directly into Publisher

This section will look at different types of images that can be created in different graphics editing packages which can then be imported into Publisher.

Information: Types of graphic

Images can be saved in different file formats like the text files discussed in Section 3. The most common picture formats are:

- .gif
- .jpeg
- .tif
- .bmp
- vector

Image format	Information
.gif	**Graphic Interchange Format** – this type of file format is most suited to drawings. When pictures are saved in this format only 256 colours are visible.
.jpeg	**Joint Photographic Experts Group** – this file format is suitable for photographs as this format uses 16 million colours and the files are a smaller size than .gif.
.tif	**Tagged Image File** – image files are compressed without affecting the quality.
.bmp	**Bitmap** – bitmap graphics are often photographs and the format doesn't allow much manipulation – you can alter the size and shape of a bitmap graphic, however the more you play with the image the more the appearance suffers. Usually bitmap images use Microsoft paint software.
Vector	**Vector** – vector graphics are picture formats which can be easily sized and shaped whilst retaining the quality and appearance. Vector files are also known as raster files and generally hold very graphical, non-phototype images, e.g. cartoons or line drawings.

Method

1. Create a new folder and name it **images**.
2. Load **Microsoft Paint** – then open **Start**, **Programs**, **Accessories**, **Paint**.
3. Create logo by drawing an ellipse.

Figure 7.1 Paint toolbox

4. Add the text **Fleur Today**.
5. Add a pale yellow fill effect.
6. Save the file as **flogo** as a .bmp file in the **images** folder.
7. Print one copy of the file and close the file.

Information: Copyright

In a publication, copyright covers the content and the design elements of the work. This covers the style, composition, layout and general appearance of a published work. The copyright of a work usually rests with the author or creator of the work and usage of copyright material therefore requires the permission from the copyright owner.

Information: Scanner

A scanner captures paper-based text/images and converts these into digital formats. Scanners come in a range of resolutions and the higher the resolution the better the quality of capture. Scanners are set up so that pictures/photographs can be placed directly onto the scanner and scanned into a graphics editing package or directly into Publisher. A flat-bed scanner is the best to use for desktop publishing as it offers high quality resolution and is ideal for copying images from books.

Task 7.2 — Scanning an image into a graphics editor

You will need to ask your tutor for support during this activity as there are many different types of scanner and editing software.

Method

1 Select a suitable picture and place this face down on your scanner.
2 Scan the picture into the software using the instructions provided by your tutor.
3 Save a copy of the image to your **images** folder.
4 Open Publisher and create a new blank publication.
5 Draw a box with the **Picture Frame** tool 🖼.
6 The Insert Picture dialogue box automatically opens.
7 Open the **images** folder and insert the picture you have scanned into the computer.
8 Save the publication as **scan** and close the file.

Information: Scanning into Publisher

Images can be scanned directly into Publisher instead of into your graphics editing software.

Task 7.3 — Scan directly into Publisher

Method

1 Turn on your scanner and place the picture you want to scan on it.
2 Open Publisher and create a picture frame using the **Picture Frame** tool.
3 Click **Insert**, **Picture**, and select **From Scanner or Camera**. In the **Insert Picture From Scanner or Camera** dialogue box, select your scanner from the Device list.
4 Start the scanning process using your scanner and make any adjustments you want to the scanned image.
5 When you're finished, exit the scanning program and the scanned image is added to the publication.
6 Save the publication as **scan1** and close the publication.

Information: Capturing a picture

Images can be captured from cameras and camcorders into graphics editing software. The photographs can be 'touched up' to remove any scratches or 'red-eye', or you can increase the brightness or colours to increase the quality of the image.

Task 7.4 — Capturing a picture

Method

1 Select a suitable photograph from your camera or camcorder.
2 Using the software that came with your camera attach the camera to the computer using the instructions provided by your tutor to capture the photograph.
3 Save a copy of the image to your **images** folder.
4 Open Publisher and create a new blank publication.
5 Draw a box with the **Picture Frame** tool.
6 The Insert Picture dialogue box automatically opens.
7 Open the **images** folder and insert the picture you have scanned into the computer.
8 Save the publication as **scan** and close the file.

Information: Capture a picture in Publisher

Instead of capturing a photo from your camera into your camera software, Publisher allows you to import the images directly into the software. One thing to consider is the size of the image file and the memory this will take up on your computer.

Task 7.5 — Capture a picture in Publisher

Method

1 Make sure your camera is attached to your computer, and that any necessary software for your camera is installed.
2 Click on the **Insert** menu, point to **Picture**, point to **From Scanner or Camera**, and then click.
3 Using the camera's program, start the capture process and make any adjustments you want to the image.
4 When you're finished, exit the camera program.
5 Create a text box and add your name and today's date beneath the picture you have captured.
6 Add appropriate border art to your picture.
7 Save a copy of the publication as **camera2** in the images folder.

→ Practise your skills 1 – Drawing a logo

1 Load **Microsoft Paint** and create a new logo.
2 The logo should be a rounded rectangle.
3 Add the text **MyOrg.com**.
4 Add a pale blue fill effect.
5 Save the file as **mylogo** as a Windows bitmap file in the **images** folder and print one copy.
6 Close the file and exit Microsoft Paint.

→ Practise your skills 2 – Scan into Publisher

1 Turn on your scanner and place the picture you want to scan on it.
2 Open Publisher and create a picture frame using the **Picture Frame** tool.
3 Insert the picture and start the scanning process using your scanner.
4 Exit the scanning program and the scanned image is added to the publication.
5 Save the publication as **scan2** in the **images** folder and close the publication.

→ Practise your skills 3 – Capture in Publisher

1 Make sure your camera is attached to your computer.
2 Draw a picture frame and acquire the image from your camera.
3 Using the camera's program, start the scanning process.
4 Save a copy of the publication as **photo2** in the **images** folder.

→ Check your knowledge

1 What is meant by the term 'scanner'?
2 How does a scanner transfer paper-based documents into an electronic format?
3 What is the difference between a vector and a bitmap image?
4 What does copyright mean when using images created by someone else?
5 How can a graphics editor enhance your image?
6 How does resolution affect the level of detail of an image?

Section 8 | Manipulating images

You will learn to

- Adjust brightness and contrast
- Edit graphics to modify colour, fill and style
- Use guides to position/align graphic elements
- Add and remove layout guides
- Anchor graphics
- Add background colour

This section looks at images that have been inserted into a publication and how these images can be manipulated or the quality enhanced to produce a more professional publication.

Information: Brightness and contrast

Brightness in images determines the number of shades that are shown on an image where contrast determines the intensity of the shades of colour. A high contrast image has less grey shades and has less visible details whereas an image with low contrast has more grey shades. By adjusting the brightness and contrast of an image you can balance the overall tones of the picture and bring out the detail of the image. The brightness control adds or subtracts colour from each pixel (the smallest part of images are built up comprising hundreds/thousands of pixels) to make the image look brighter or darker. The contrast stretches or condenses the spectrum of colours.

Information: Edit graphic to modify colour and fill style

Images can be modified or colours changed to make your publication look more individual and professional. Using Publisher you can change the colour of clip art images, add tints, fills or pattern effects.

Tints

Fills

Gradient fills

Method

1 Create a new folder named **amends**.
2 Create a new publication then draw a **clip art frame** and insert a suitable image from **Clip Art**.
3 On the **Format** menu, select the Picture tab and then the **Recolor...** button (Figure 8.1).
4 Click the arrow next to **Color** (see Figure 8.2).

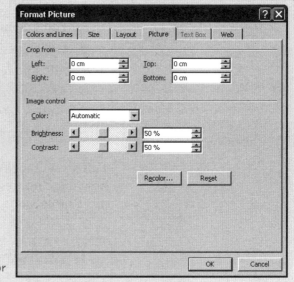

Figure 8.1 Recolor

5 Select **More Colors** and choose blue. Click **OK**. (see Figure 8.2).

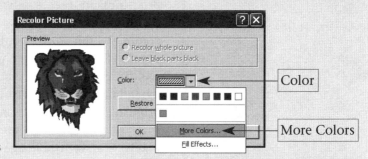

Figure 8.2 More Colors

6 Click the arrow next to **Colour:** again and choose **Fill Effects**. Select the **20%** tint (see Figure 8.3) and click **OK**.

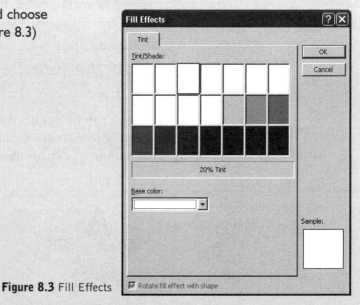

Figure 8.3 Fill Effects

7 Click on **Color** and change the colour to **blue**.
8 Click **Apply** and click **OK** twice. The image should now have changed to blue in colour.
9 Save the publication as **blue** in the **amends** folder and close the publication.

Task 8.2 — Edit clip art and adjust the brightness/contrast

The brightness/contrast of an image in Publisher is changed by editing the picture without having to leave Publisher.

Method

1. Open the **blue** publication and select the picture.
2. Edit the picture by increasing the brightness (click the icon about five times) – see Figure 8.4.

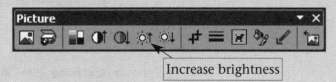

Increase brightness

Figure 8.4 Picture toolbar

3. When you've finished editing the picture, click anywhere in the Publisher workspace and the picture toolbar will disappear.
4. Save the publication as **blue1** into the **amends** folder and close the file.

Information: Layout guides

Layout guides allow you to place your image accurately on the page. In Publisher the layout guides show a grid which allows you to organise text, pictures and objects into columns and rows to provide a consistent appearance to your publication. Layout guides are represented in the publication by the blue and pink dotted lines and you can use them to align different objects in a publication.

Task 8.3 — Adding and removing layout guides using the ruler

Hint:

To remove layout guides:
1. On the **Arrange** menu, click **Layout Guides**.
2. Under **Grid Guides**, change the number of columns and rows to 1.
3. If you've changed the margins and want to reset them, under **Margin Guides** select the options you want.

Method

1. Create a new publication and insert three clip art images.
2. Using the rulers place the mouse pointer onto the left ruler, hold down the **Shift** key and drag the ruler to the left of the first image.
3. Click **Arrange, Snap to Ruler Marks**.
4. Drag each of the images close to the ruler guide and they will snap into position exactly where you want them.
5. Save the publication as **rule** in the **amends** folder and close the publication.

Task 8.4 | Anchor a graphic

Method

1   Create a new publication, **A4 portrait** with default margins and draw a text frame within the blue guides.
2   Key in the following text:
    Internet Banking
    With Internet banking you are able to check your balance, transfer funds or create new direct debits yourself using the bank's online facility, and some banks are offering this service via mobile phone technology!
    This means that you no longer have to queue during your lunch hour and find that when you get to the front of the queue the computers have crashed! You can access your account 24 hours a day, seven days a week.
3   Insert a suitable clip art image by drawing the frame on top of the first paragraph of text.
4   Click on **Insert**, **Picture**, **Clip Art** and insert a suitable image.
5   To group both the text and image together select both the text and picture frames by holding down the **Shift** key and selecting both frames.
6   Click **Arrange, Group**.

   A group button [graphic] is shown at the bottom right of the selection box.

   A single set of selection handles surrounds the whole group and you can move both the text and image frames as one item.
7   Save the publication as **group** and close the publication.

→ Practise your skills 1

1 Create a new publication, **A4 portrait** with default margins and single column layout.

2 You are going to produce a new front cover for a safety leaflet to be used on transatlantic flights (see layout below).

3 Insert the headline

   JET AIRCRAFT

   as a separate text box which is shown across box columns of text.

4 Draw a clip art gallery frame and insert a suitable colour image from Clip Art.

5 Apply a **blue** and **white** gradient fill selecting the first gradient fill effect from the toolbox.

6 Change the colour of the image to **grey**.

7 Align the graphic with the text using Publisher's **Snap to** function.

8 Add the following text:

   Aircraft

   Emergency

   Procedures

   These procedures have been updated in line with consultation from both the UK and USA governments.

9 Anchor the heading and graphic, and group as one object.

10 Apply suitable text styles/enhancements to the publication.

11 Save the publication as **jet** and print one copy of the publication before closing the file.

   Layout for Practise your skills 1

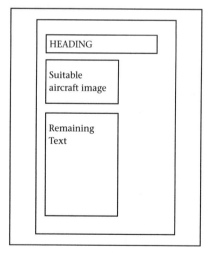

→ Practise your skills 2

1 Create a new publication, **A4 portrait** with default margins and two column layout.

2 You are going to produce a new front cover for a safety leaflet as to the risk of fire to be used for staff working in hotels (see layout below).

3 Create a text frame and key in the headline

FIRE RISKS IN HOTELS

4 Draw a clip art gallery frame and insert a suitable fire safety colour image from Clip Art.

5 Apply a **red** and **white** gradient fill selecting the first gradient fill effect from the toolbox.

6 Change the colour of the image to **blue**.

7 Align the graphic with the right-hand side of the heading using Publisher's **Snap to** function.

8 Add the following text:

This new publication has been produced to comply with recent changes in health and safety legislation and will help you to assist our customers, should a fire start.

9 Anchor the graphic and text, and group as one object.

10 Apply suitable text styles and emphasis to the publication.

11 Save the publication as **fire**, print one copy and close the publication.

Layout for Practise your skills 2

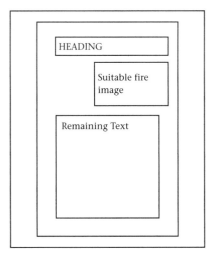

→ Check your knowledge

1 What are the benefits of anchoring images?

2 Why do you use layout/grids to place items?

3 List two fill effects that you could use.

4 What is brightness/contrast?

Section 9 | Attributes or properties of an image

You will learn to

- Size images
- Set the shape of an image
- Add borders
- Add a frame or a caption to an image
- Overlay text on an image (wrapping)
- Flip/mirror, scale, rotate and crop to graphic object

In this section we will look at editing graphics in greater depth.

Information: Size of images

Images can be reduced or increased in size to create a more balanced appearance to your publication. In Publisher you can change the size of images by using the selection handles or by keying in the exact specifications. When you resize images it is important to maintain the image's original proportions otherwise the image can become distorted. The first image below has been resized proportionally and the second image has not been resized proportionally to show how distorted the image can become.

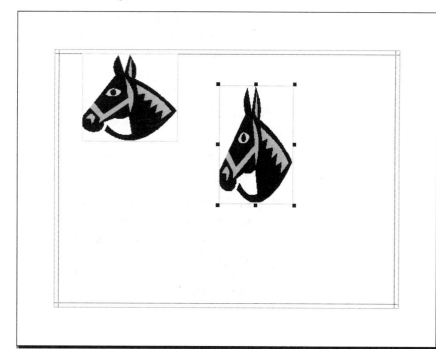

Figure 9.1 Example of resized images

Method

1 Open the publication **jet** from the **amends** folder and resize the image by dragging the lower left selection handle to increase the size of the image (see Figure 9.2) to an approximate size of **10 cm wide by 8 cm tall**. (**Note:** You will have to remove the anchor to do this.)

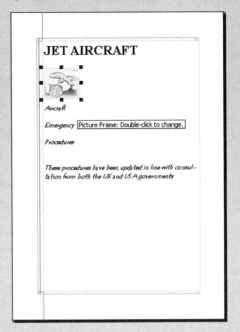

Figure 9.2 Selection handles

2 Save the publication as **jet1**.
3 Now resize the image using exact measurements of **9 cm × 4.55 cm**. To do this select the image and click on **Format, Picture, Size** and enter the values in the **Height and Width** boxes.
4 Change the colour of the image to purple.
5 Increase the size of the body text so that it fills the page.
6 Save the publication as **jet2** and close the file.

Information: Change the shape of custom images

In Publisher you can change the shape of an image that you have drawn using the **AutoShapes** tool. This tool only applies to images that have been created using the Custom Shapes tool.

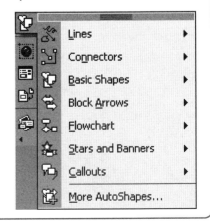

Figure 9.3 AutoShapes tool

Task 9.2 | Setting the shape of an image

Method

1. Create a new A4 landscape publication using the default settings.
2. Click on the **Custom Shapes** tool and draw a cross (see Figure 9.4).

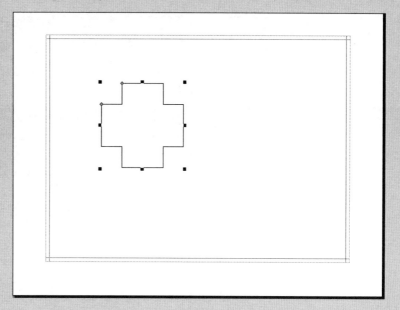

Figure 9.4 Cross shape

3. Ensure that the shape is still selected and position the mouse pointer over an Adjust handle (grey diamond-shaped selection handles) until you see the Adjust pointer.
4. Hold down the mouse button and drag the handle to change the shape until it looks like that in Figure 9.5 below. You will need to do both the horizontal and vertical sizing.

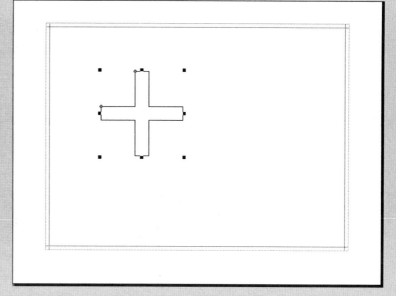

Figure 9.5 New shape

5. Close the file without saving.

> **Information:** Adding borders
>
> We have already looked at adding borders in Section 1. The same principle applies in that borders or border art can be added to images and shadows can be applied to enhance the images within your publication.

Task 9.3 Adding a border to an image

Method

1 Open the publication **fire** and select the picture. Right-click on the image that you had inserted earlier and select **Format Picture colors and lines.**

2 To add a line border click **Line Color:** and change to Black. Click **4pt** and as a **box**. Click **OK.**

3 Add a border to the text frame using the **Checkered Box** design from **Border Art**. Right-click on the text frame and select **Format Text Box, Border Art.**

4 Scroll down the list until you reach **Checkered Bar**, click **OK** twice and the border style will be applied to the text frame.

5 Save the publication as **fire2**, print one copy of the publication and close the file.

> **Information:** Add a caption to an image
>
> To make images more interesting you can add a caption or frame.

Task 9.4 Add a caption

Method

1 Create a new publication and insert a clip art image of a telephone.

2 Draw an autoshape of a callout box – see Figure 9.6.

Figure 9.6 Callouts

3 Create a text box in the caption shape and add the text **Good Morning**.

4 Save the file as **callout** and close the file.

Task 9.5 — Overlay text and images

Method

1. Open the publication **blue** from the **amends** folder.
2. Create a text box over the image and key in the following text:

   ADOPT A LION

   Today you can adopt a lion for less than £1 per day.

   Lions are disappearing so fast from parts of Africa they could soon become extinct. As farming spreads throughout west and central Africa, the World Conservation Union says lions' habitats are disappearing fast but the big cats are also being killed off by poisoning and hunting which is still legal in some countries.

   Your adoption helps towards the upkeep of the animal so if you have always wanted to look after a Lion but were afraid it would eat the cat, this is the next best thing!

   Contact us today for further information!

3. The text will be placed onto the image and at this point you may be unable to see the image.
4. Click on the **Send to Back** drop down button 🖼 on the **Standard** toolbar.
5. The picture should be visible.
6. The text will now be over the image. Change the text to a suitable **serif** font and increase the size of the body text and ensure that the text is clearly visible over the image. Change the heading **Adopt a Lion** by double-clicking in the **WordArt** frame and then choosing the **wave** design. Add a border and fill effects to this shape.
7. Add your name and today's date using a superscript.
8. Save the publication as **lion**, print one copy and close the publication.

> **Hint:**
>
> Sometimes the text frame has a white fill effect and you need to make this transparent so that the picture is visible behind the text. To do this click **Ctrl+T** and the picture will be visible behind the text.

Information: Wrap text

When an image has been inserted you may wish to wrap the text around the image instead of having the text directly above or below it. Text can be wrapped around images, word art objects, text or tables.

Text can be wrapped as irregular text wrap, wrapped to frame or wrapped to picture.

Irregular text wrap

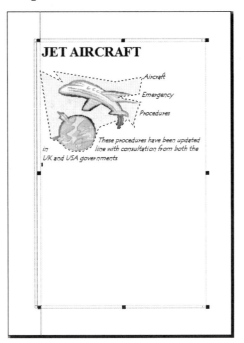

Wrap to text frame

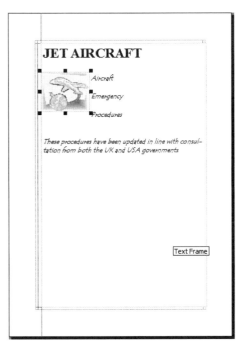

Wrap text to picture

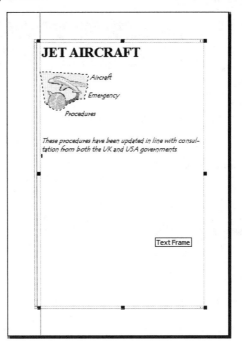

When using the text wrapping option in Publisher, the wrap automatically sets the picture frame margins at 0.00 and these can be increased depending on the amount of white space you require between the image and the text.

Hint:

If using the irregular text wrap, you will need to use **Bring to the front** on the picture. You can adjust the irregular text wrapping boundary by clicking on any of the adjust handles located at the verticals of the text boundary. As the boundary becomes more irregular, the number of adjust handles are increased.

Task 9.6   Wrap text around an image

Method

1 Create a new publication, **A4 portrait** default margins.
2 Create a text box and insert the text file **theatre1**.
3 Create a picture frame starting under the heading.
4 Insert a suitable image from **Clip Art**.
5 Right-click on the image and click **Format Picture**, **Layout** and the dialogue box in Figure 9.7 is shown.
6 Click **Wrap text**, **Both sides**.
7 Move the image to the right-hand side of the text.
8 Save the publication as **gifts**, print one copy and close the publication.

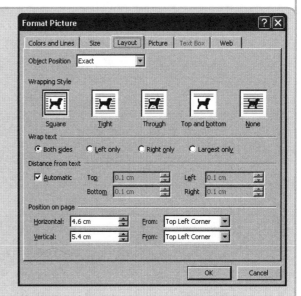

Figure 9.7 Wrap text

Note: To perform an irregular text wrap, select the Picture toolbar, click on the wrap button and select Edit Wrap Points (Figure 9.8).

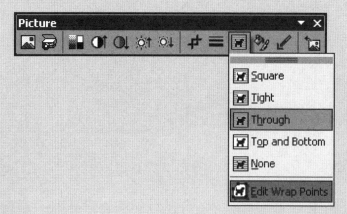

Figure 9.8 Text Wrapping

Information: Flip/mirror, scale, rotate and crop to graphic object

Once you have inserted your image into your publication you can rotate or flip the object to add visual interest to your page or to make the objects of the publication fit together better. You can rotate an object by using the selection handles or by entering an exact number into the Rotate Objects dialogue box. Flipping an object means that you can invert it vertically (e.g. top to bottom) or horizontally (left to right).

Task 9.7	**Rotate image manually**

Method

1   Open the publication **design** and insert a suitable image.
2   Rotate the image manually using the rotate selection handle. Point the mouse at the middle green selection handle (see Figure 9.9).

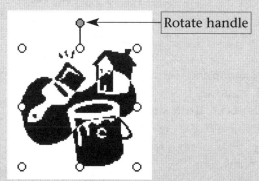

Figure 9.9 Selection handles

3   Holding down the **Alt** key rotate the image.
4   Save the publication as **rotate** and close the publication.

Note: The image can be rotated using the specific measurements and this can be found on pages 34 and 35.

Task 9.8   Flip an object

Method

1   Open the file rotate and select the image.
2   Click on the **Flip Horizontal** toolbar button ![icon]![icon] . From the **Free Rotate** ![icon] ▾ button on the standard toolbar (Figure 9.10)

Figure 9.10 Free Rotate icon

3   Save the publication as **design1** and close the file.

Information: Crop an image

The Crop Picture tool allows you to cut out certain parts of the graphic.

Task 9.9   Crop a graphic object

Method

1   Create a new publication **A4 portrait** using the default settings.
2   Draw a picture frame in the top half of the publication. Insert a similar clip art image to that shown below in Figure 9.11.

Figure 9.11 Coffee cup and steam

3 Using the Crop Picture tool ⌗ remove the steam from the cup so only the cup is left (see Figure 9.12).

Figure 9.12 Coffee cup without steam

4 Save the publication as **coffee** and close the file.

→ Practise your skills 1

1 Open the publication **coffee** and move the image to the bottom right of the publication.

2 Resize the image so that it is **9 cm** wide × **5 cm** high.

3 Create a word art frame at the top of the publication and key in the heading **INTERNET CAFÉ**.

4 Create a text frame to fill the rest of the publication and click **Send to Back** so that the coffee cup image is shown. Remember you may need to make the background transparent.

Key in the following text:

Our new internet café is open 7 days a week between the hours of 10 am and 10 pm.

Each computer is linked up via Broadband allowing high speed access and costs just £2 for 20 minutes of access.

Strict terms and conditions must be adhered to and these will be provided on request.

Our dedicated staff are trained to provide help and support and we have a technician on site should problems occur.

Why not visit us and find out more!

5 Increase the size of the text so that it fills the page, using a **serif** font.

→

6 Insert a clip art frame starting at **Each computer ...** and insert a suitable clip art image of a computer and ensure that the size of this frame is set to **3cm** × **3cm**. **Wrap text to frame**. Ensure that all text and images are shown.

7 Save a copy of the publication as **café** and print one copy of the file.

8 Rotate the computer image **270°** and align this to the right side of the text frame.

9 Increase the size of the text frame so that it fills the whole page.

10 Change the wrap text to picture and create an irregular wrap text by changing some of the wrap points.

11 Save the publication as **internet** and print one copy of the file.

12 Close the publication.

→ Check your knowledge

1 What is the difference between wrap text to frame and irregular text wrap around an image?

2 Why should you resize a picture in proportion?

3 Why would you overlay text/images?

4 Why would you flip an image?

Section 10 | Copyfit a publication

You will learn to

- Identify white space
- Adjust line spacing
- Adjust leading/kerning
- Insert hyphenation
- Insert rules
- Identify a symmetric/asymmetric layout

In this section you will learn how to copyfit a publication so that it is ready for printing

Information: White space

The areas around graphics/text and at all sides of the page or columns are known as white space. When designing your publication you should think about the use of the printed material and the readers that it may attract. This should influence your master setup and how much white space you should leave around text and image boxes.

Publications look more professional when items are aligned at the top and bottom of columns and where there is not more than 10 mm of white space anywhere in the publication. This can be achieved by

- enlarging or reducing the size of any graphics
- adjusting the line spacing
- adjusting the leading
- adjusting the size and appearance of text (unless specified in the assignment).

Information: Line and character spacing

Text is generally printed in single, double or 1.5 line spacing which helps the reader to read the text but also enhances the display of the document.

The following are examples of line spacing:

This is an example of text which has been typed in single line spacing. Notice how little space there is between the lines.

This is an example of text which has been typed in double line spacing. Notice how there is one

clear line space between each line of printed text.

This is an example of text which has been typed in 1.5 line spacing. Notice how the space

between each line of text is smaller than the double.

Method

1. Create a new publication with **A4 portrait** orientation, margins of **3 cm** all round and **one** column of text.
2. Create a text box to fill the area created and insert the text file **bags1**.
3. Publisher will automatically default the line spacing to single spacing. To change the line spacing to double, highlight all the text you have keyed in, click **Format**, **Line Spacing** and the dialogue box in Figure 10.1 will be displayed.

Figure 10.1 Line Spacing

4. Change the **Between lines** spacing to **2 sp** by clicking on the up arrow to increase the spacing. Click **OK**.
5. The text will now be displayed in double line spacing.
6. Save the publication as **bags** and close the file.

Information: Leading and kerning

Leading is the term given to the exact spacing between lines of text. The leading can be adjusted to give different effects on the page but can also be used to reduce the amount of visible white space. It is important that leading is consistent for each different style within a publication, e.g. the leading of all body text should be consistent but this can be different to the leading before and after subheadings.

Kerning is the term given to space between characters – this may also be known as 'tracking'. In Publisher the setting of the tracking default is **normal**. The following is an example of kerning:

| Example 1 – tracking – normal |
| Example 2 – t r a c k i n g – expand |
| Example 3 – tracking – condense |

Method

1　Open the **gifts** publication and print one copy.
2　Highlight all of the text to change the character spacing to **tight** by clicking on the **Format**, **Character Spacing** menu and the dialogue box in Figure 10.2 is shown.

Figure 10.2 Character Spacing

3　Decrease the **kerning** by condensing the space between the characters to **1.5 pt**.
4　Increase the **leading** by changing the before and after point size to **1.5 pt**.
5　Save the publication as **gifts1** and print out one copy and examine each printout for the difference in the character spacing.

Information: Hyphenation

In Publisher the hyphenation of words is set on automatically, which means that if you have text and images aligned to the right margin or right columns with a lot of hyphens shown, then this makes the work look untidy and sometimes difficult to read. Publications look more professional with hyphenation switched off.

Task 10.3   Hyphenation

Method

1. Open the publication **cook** and select the body text frame.
2. On the **Tools** menu, point to **Language**, and then click **Hyphenation**.
3. Click the **Automatically hyphenate this story** check box to remove the tick.
4. Save the publication as **hyphen** and close the file.

Information: Rules

Rules can be used to separate text or give prominence to headings and can divide the space. Rules are lines that can be drawn using the line tool in Publisher. Different thickness of lines can be used throughout a publication, however for consistency the same weight of line should be used throughout.

Task 10.4   Ruled lines

Method

1. Open the Publication **internet** and draw a line underneath the heading and above the body text frame.
2. Click on the **Line** tool (see Figure 10.3) and draw the line using the 'cross-hair'.
3. To obtain a straight line hold down the **Shift** key whilst drawing the line.

Figure 10.3 Line tool

4. Right-click on the line, select **Format, AutoShape** and change this to a **4pt** size.
5. Save the publication as **rules**, print one copy and close the publication.

Information: Symmetry/asymmetry

The Publication layout design can be symmetric (centred) or asymmetric (off-centre). A centred publication would be appropriate for a novel where the layout is static and the items on the page can be balanced, for example by putting illustrations in each corner. An asymmetric publication is where items do not have to be balanced and where columns can be left blank.

→ Practise your skills 1

1 Create a new publication with **A4 portrait** orientation with **2** columns and **2 cm** margins all round.

2 Key in the following text in **12 pt** size:

Property of the Week

Would you like to live in a Grade II listed cottage with thatched roof and original features? We have the ideal property for you.

The property features a long drive leading up to the front of the property with large solid wooden gates which provide a secure garden and off road parking. A single garage with up and over door is provided next to the property which features a fenced area of lawn, a pergola over decking crossing the village stream and paved courtyard.

The property has accommodation on two floors and on entering the property you find yourself in the sitting room which features an inglenook fireplace over a flagstone hearth. The inglenook has space for a log store, seating and a small shelved open cupboard. The beams are exposed to the ceiling and there is a large window featuring a window seat. Double doors lead into the dining room with fireplace and views across the village green.

The kitchen and breakfast room provide a built-in pantry with larder and the utility room houses the washing machine and dishwasher and access to the loft area, and a stable door to the rear garden.

The master bedroom has a high ceiling into the eaves and exposed crossbeams. The original bedroom door opens into a dressing room with built in wardrobes and there is an en-suite bathroom and access to the loft space. Two further bedrooms have similar high ceilings and share a family bathroom.

3 Insert a suitable image from Clip Art in the bottom right column ensuring that the picture is approximately **4.75 cm x 5.50 cm**.

4 Change the line spacing so that the publication is displayed using **double** line spacing.

5 Change the heading **Property of the Week** to be displayed in a **sans serif** font, **20 pt** size, **bold** and **centred** across the first column only.

6 Increase the before and after leading space so that there is **less than 1 cm** of white space visible in the document.

7 Amend the kerning by using **Expand** and increasing the space between the characters.

8 Turn off the hyphenation in the publication.

9 Proofread the publication carefully, save the file as **house1** and print one copy.

10 Close the file.

→ Check your knowledge

1 What does symmetry mean?

2 What is meant by leading?

3 What is meant by kerning?

4 Why would you want to remove hyphenation?

5 How should you consider white space when producing a publication ?

Consolidation 2

1 Create a new publication, A4 portrait with default margins and using a two column layout.

2 Key in the headline using WordArt:

Gulet Boats

3 Draw a clip art gallery frame and insert a suitable colour boat image from Clip Art centred across both columns.

4 Create a text frame the size of the page and apply a blue and white gradient fill selecting the first gradient fill effect from the toolbox.

5 Change the colour of the image to grey.

6 Align the graphic with the text using Publisher's Snap to function.

7 Add the following text:

Why not cruise around Crete in a stylish Gulet Boat?

These boats are spacious with four air conditioned cabins, with double beds and each with en-suite facilities.

The boats include a lounge area away from the rays of the sun with a comfortable dining area on the front deck.

The boats can be hired with a crew of four including a captain to make your cruise extra special!

Once on board you can enjoy our extra facilities of a motor-board, canoe or windsurfing!

8 Anchor the heading and graphic and group as one object.

Apply suitable text styles/enhancements to the publication. The text **Why not cruise around Crete in a stylish Gulet Boat?** can be formatted in a different font to the remainder of the publication text.

9 Save the publication as **gulet** and print one copy of the publication before closing the file.

10 Move the image to the middle of the publication.

11 Resize the image so that it fills most of the column.

12 Overlay the text on the image.

13 Increase the size of the text so that it fills most of the page, using a sans serif font.

14 Insert a smaller image of a boat in the bottom right corner and rotate the boat image 90^0 and align this to the right side of the text frame.

15 Save the publication as **boat1** and print one copy of the file.

16 Decrease the kerning by condensing the space between the characters to 1.5 pt.

17 Increase the leading by changing the before and after point size to 1.5 pt.

18 Save the publication as **boat2** and print out one copy.

19 Close the file.

Section 11 | Colour separation

You will learn to

- Use RGB
- Use CMYK
- Use pantone
- Use DIC focoltone

In this section we will look at colour separation and colour printing.

Information: RGB and CMYK

Desktop publishing offers two colour models: RGB (additive) and CMYK (subtractive). Each pixel of colour that is shown on the monitor is made up of three basic colours – RGB, which stands for Red, Green and Blue. By using these three colours up to 16 million different colours can be created. Each colour on a printer is made up from three different colours and uses the CMYK, which uses Cyan, Magenta, Yellow and Black to produce a range of colours.

Use of colour can provide emphasis, visual impact, identity and a professional finish to a document.

Information: Pantone

Pantone is a defined set of standard colours for printing, each of which is specified by a single number and available in a swatch book. Publisher uses the pantone number system for spot-colour printing. You may find that your computer monitor can only show some of the colours, however, when the publication is printed by using colour separation a different pantone colour is produced, enabling a print shop to exactly reproduce the original desired colour.

Task 11.1 | Setting up for colour printing

Method

1 Open the publication **rules** and set up the publication for process-colour printing. To do this click on **Tools**, **Commercial Printing Tools**, and **Color Printing**.
2 In the **Print all colors** as box, click **Process colors CMYK** and click **OK**.
3 Save the publication as **CMYK** and close the publication.

Information: DIC and focoltone

DIC is the brand name of a colour matching system produced by Dai Nippon Ink & Chemicals, Inc. This uses a number range of coloured inks.

Focoltone is a colour matching system which was produced by Focoltone International. This uses a range of coloured inks which are specified and identified by a number which is then reproduced by a professional printing company.

In Publisher you can compare the printer and screen colours by printing a colour sampler. This depends on the desktop printer and the print settings you select, and this will determine the colours in the printed publication which might differ from the colours you see on the screen. Printing a colour sampler before you design your publication will help you decide what colours will work best with your printer.

Task 11.2	Selecting colour scheme

Method

1	Open the **internet** publication.
2	On the **Format** menu, click **Color Schemes**.
3	In the **Color Schemes** task pane click **Custom color scheme**, click the **Standard** tab, then click **Print color sampler** and click **OK**.
4	Close the file without saving any changes.

Information: Colour separation

When your publication is printed, the colours are printed separately so that when you print a one page, two colour publication, two pages will be printed – one for the first colour and one for the second colour.

Information: Spot colour

Work that is printed out as a spot colour is where the ink colour is separated and printed on its own plate. For example, you can select the colour you wish to use as a spot colour from the colours provided in Publisher, e.g. red, and then when you print you only print text/images that have been applied with the red ink colour. Spot colour allows commercial full-colour print output to be recreated by passing the paper through the printer's press one for each spot colour. Once you have chosen your spot colour you can apply it to the text or to drawn objects and imported bitmaps to ensure that they are output to the correct colour plate. This method of printing is more economical when you use one or two colour plates.

Information: Typesetting

Before computers were used for typesetting, books were typeset by placing lead type into a form. Kerning entailed shaving lead off a character and leading was used by placing extra lead between the lines of type. Today technology has taken over and the typesetting uses a computer-generated layout and design of a text to produce the finished product ready for printing.

Task 11.3 Separating colours

Method

I   Open the publication **design1** and change the first line of text to a red font colour and change the last line of text in the publication to a red font colour.
2   Click on **Tools, Commercial Printing Tools**, select **Color Printing** and then **Spot Color**. Click **OK**.
3   Click on the **File, Print**. The print dialogue box is shown (see Figure 11.1).

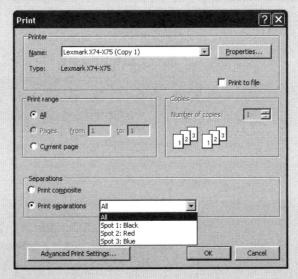

Figure 11.1 Print dialogue box

4   Click on the **Print separations** option and select **Spot 1: Black** from the drop-down list. The text in black will be printed on a page on its own.
5   To print the black text on its own, go back, select **File, Print, Print separations** and **Black**.
6   Mark on each printout which colour has been printed.
7   Save the file as **design2** and close the file.

→ Practise your skills 1

1 Use the publication **house1**.
2 Change the title **Property of the Week** and the clip art image to a **blue** spot colour and ensure that the remaining body text has a **black** spot colour applied.
3 Produce a separate printout, first showing the blue text and image.
4 Produce a further printout showing the text in black.
5 Mark on each printout which colour has been printed.
6 Save the file as **house2** and close the file.

→ Check your knowledge

1 What is meant by CMYK?
2 What is the pantone matching system?
3 What is focoltone?
4 What is spot colour?
5 What is meant by typesetting?
6 Why do differences in colour arise between the screen and final printed output?

Print and file output considerations

You will learn to

- Print preview
- Proof your publication
- Use scale versions
- Use crop marks
- Select print output resolution, copies, size
- Select bitmap and scaleable fonts
- Select printer and screen fonts

In this final section we will look at the different print options that are available to you.

Information: Print preview and proofing process

It is imperative that you proof your publication before sending it to print. This will ensure that you print a correct document so that you save on the paper and ink of the printout. Publisher will show you what the finished product will look like. A draft print of the publication can be produced (you will need to ask your tutor for details for your printer).

In Publisher you can use the design checker which can identify any possible design mistakes.

Task 12.1 | Using the design checker

Method

1 Open the publication **design2** and click on **Tools**, **Design Checker**. Ensure that **All** is checked and click **OK**.
2 The design checker will identify problems, e.g. 'There were two spaces after a punctuation mark.' At this point you can make changes to your publication following the suggestions made by the design checker. If you don't want to make any of the changes suggested click on **ignore**.
3 Click **OK** when the design check is complete.
4 Close the publication without saving any changes.

Hint:

If the design checker makes a suggestion which you are unsure of click on the **Explain** button for additional information.

Information: Scale versions

Scale versions allow you to produce a smaller version of the original publication, e.g. 50% of the original size, to save on the printing process.

Information: Crop marks

Crop marks are small lines that appear when your publication is a different size to the piece of paper you are printing on and they indicate how the printed pages should be trimmed so that they can be correctly assembled in your publication.

Task 12.2 | Using crop marks

Method

Remember:

To turn off crop marks, clear the **Crop marks** check box.

1 Open the publication **practice1** and click **File** and **Print**.
2 Click **Advanced Print Settings**.
3 In the **Publication Options** dialogue box, under **Printer's marks**, select the **Crop marks** check box.
4 Click **OK** twice.

Information: Output (resolution, copies)

In Publisher images can be printed in either high or low resolution linked graphics. If you select to print low resolution graphics this will affect the final quality printout of your publication and some of the quality will be lost in the reproduction.

In Publisher you can also change the number of copies of printouts that can be made and this can be selected from the Print dialogue box.

Information: Fonts

Hint:

To embed a font click on **Tools, Commercial Printing Tools** and select **Fonts**. Click the check box to embed TrueType fonts into the publication.

In Publisher the publication doesn't contain the fonts; it contains instructions that refer to fonts installed in your computer system. If you use unusual fonts that a printing company does not have then different fonts will be substituted at the time of printing. Publisher embeds TrueType fonts into your publication so that when you take it to the professional printing company a special dialogue box allows the fonts to be temporarily installed for the purpose of printing the publication.

A bitmap font is a font where each character is saved as an array of pixels (bitmap) where the fonts are not scaleable.

A scaleable font is where the font can be increased or reduced within a range of sizes without distorting the final effect.

Task 12.3 · Using the font scheme

Method

1. Open the publication **jet2** from the **amends** folder and select **Tools**, **Commercial Printing Tools**, **Color Printing** and select the options you want.
2. Click **Format** and **Font Scheme**.
3. In the **Font Scheme** dialogue box, click a font scheme.

> **Information:** Set properties for your desktop printer
>
> Because printers differ with regard to options such as resolution, font settings, and colour, the options available in the **Properties** dialogue box will vary from one printer to another. Ask your tutor to consult your printer manual for information about your printer's capabilities, the exact name of the option you want, and where it's located in the **Properties** dialogue box.
>
> For a printer:
> 1. On the **File** menu, click **Print**.
> 2. Click **Properties**.
> 3. Select the options you want. Click **OK** twice.
>
> For Publisher:
> 4. On the **File** menu, click **Print**, and then click **Advanced Print Settings** to set advanced options at print time.
>
> If in the case of printers you want to print only in black and white, then you need to change the settings accordingly.

→ Practise your skills 1

1. Open the **house2** publication.
2. Change the size of the page setup so that the publication paper size is now **28 cm** × **19 cm** and **landscape** orientation.
3. Apply the **Printer's Crop Marks** to the publication.
4. Select the font scheme **Economy** from Publisher's Font Scheme menu.
5. Print one copy of the publication showing the crop marks with a high resolution print.

→ Check your knowledge

1 What is the proofing process?

2 What do you need to consider when using fonts in a publication with regard to the final output?

3 What are crop marks and why would you use them?

Practice assignment

This assignment is broken down into three parts:

1 A brief scenario is provided.

2 Task A requires you to produce an electronic graphic image using a scanner or digital camera and draw a company logo.

3 Task B requires candidates to produce a sample marketing brochure on single-sided A4 paper.

Scenario

You work in the marketing department of a large internet order company – Designonline.com – and as an employee of the company you have been asked to design a sample marketing brochure for special offers.

The brochure will consist of

- pages, in portrait, to be printed as single-sided on A4 paper
- plus a front cover containing a graphical image (scanned or digital camera) and a company logo created using graphics editing software
- a running header including the title and date
- a footer containing your name and the page number
- prepared text held on disk
- a minimum of three further graphic images.

Task A

In this task you are required to produce graphics for use in the marketing brochure. This should be an electronic graphic image using a scanner or a digital camera, saved on disk and modified using graphics software. The graphic image will later be used to illustrate the front cover of the brochure. You also need to create a company logo that will be used on the front cover of the brochure.

1 Create a directory/folder and name it **Original**.

2 Start up the scanner, access the scanner software and scan an image, or capture an image with a digital camera.

3 Modify the colour balance, brightness, contrast and intensity of your graphic image as necessary, using appropriate software.

4 Save the graphic image with the filename **design cover** in the directory/folder called **Original**.

5 Use graphics editing software to create a company logo.

6 Save the company logo with the filename **designlogo** in the directory/folder **Original**.

Task B

In this task you are required to produce a mock-up of a marketing brochure for special offers. The brochure will be printed as single-sided on A4 paper.

The brochure will consist of

- single-sided A4 pages in portrait
- a front cover containing a graphic image and a company logo
- a running header including the title and date
- a footer containing your name and the page number
- sample pages to demonstrate layout and type style.

1   Key the following text into a suitable text editor and save this using a .txt format. Use the filename **details** and save in the **Original** directory/folder.

NEW FOR SPRING/SUMMER

Our new internet catalogue is now available and we are pleased to announce that we have increased our ranges and now can exclusively offer to you men's and childrenswear. As always our products offer exceptional quality, modern styling at extremely affordable prices!

Our men's and ladieswear designs have been specially created to ensure that each item offers you quality and design that you have come to expect.

Childrenswear

Our new childrenswear section includes those new additions to your family and teenagers who are looking for the ultimate in high fashion quality clothing.

Menswear

Our new menswear section has everything you need for that man in your life! From workwear to casual/weekend wear and sports outfits offering our superb quality and affordability promise.

Designer Brands

Our designer brands have increased and we are pleased to announce three new designers. The designers have been showing their fashions round the world and have decided to settle in England and offer their designs via our company.

Stock and Purchasing

You can check whether the item you want is in stock when you shop online. Just click on an item or type in the catalogue number to find out and remember you can try the goods at home before agreeing to purchase!

Remember ordering is secure and goods can be with you within 24 hours of ordering your items.

Regards

Designonline.com

2   Check the text for accuracy and save the file in the directory/folder **Original** with the filename **details**. Close the application.

3   Open the desktop publishing application, create a new publication and save it with the filename **BROCHURE** in the directory/folder **Original**.

4 Select margins, type style and size, justification and line length for the page and create a master page/style sheet for the brochure using different styles for the heading, subheadings and body text.

5 Create a running header including the title **DESIGNONLINE.COM** and the date.

6 Add *your name* and number the pages in a footer and use a rule/line to separate the footer from the body of the page.

7 Save the layout (template/master) with the filename **master** in the directory/folder **Original**.

8 Insert the following additional text before the text **Regards**.

   Remember to order before 5pm and get free delivery within 48 hours or pay £4.99 for next day delivery (except Saturday and Sunday).

9 Insert the graphic image **designcover**, created in Task A, positioned centrally on the front cover. Resize/crop to suit.

10 Insert the company logo on the front cover.

11 Import the text from the file **text** on to page 1 of the brochure to flow on to subsequent pages.

12 Insert at least *three* graphic images to illustrate the products. Wrap the appropriate text around the images and anchor them in position.

13 Preview the publication and check the layout for accuracy.

14 Print out the entire brochure in colour.

15 Save the printed output to disk with the filename **DESIGN2** in the directory/folder **Original**. Close the application. Proofread your publication and hand in to your tutor for marking.

Questions

1 Why should you check your computer's available memory (RAM) and disk storage space before beginning this assessment?

2 Why would you create your text as a .txt file?

3 The image that you will scan in will be affected by resolution – why is this?

4 (a) What does CMYK stand for?

   (b) Name a pre-defined colour scheme that can be used for two-colour printing.

   (c) Give *one* reason why differences in colour may occur between final printed output and the screen display.

5 Write down a description of *one* method suitable for volume colour printing of the brochure.

6 Write down *one* advantage of using scaleable printer fonts.

Solutions

Section 1 Revise basics

Task 1.6

Candidate Name

Activities include:

Face Painting

Gym

Free Play

Song time

Bruno Bear

Invites you to join

Our weekly activities

At Brandon Community Centre

Practise your skills 1

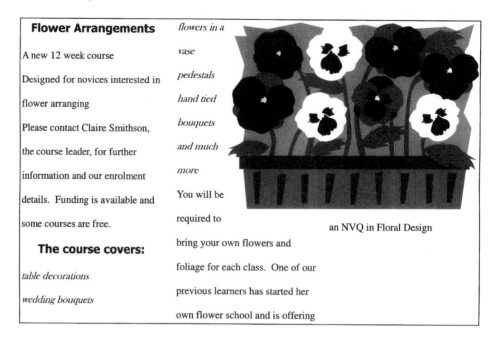

Flower Arrangements

A new 12 week course

Designed for novices interested in flower arranging

Please contact Claire Smithson, the course leader, for further information and our enrolment details. Funding is available and some courses are free.

The course covers:

table decorations

wedding bouquets

flowers in a vase

pedestals

hand tied bouquets

and much more

You will be required to bring your own flowers and foliage for each class. One of our previous learners has started her own flower school and is offering

an NVQ in Floral Design

Check your knowledge

1 Portrait and landscape.

2 The space between two columns.

3 Line or border art.

4 A low resolution copy would be draft copy which would save on the ink and could be used to proofread the publication.

5 A publication printed to file would be used later by a printing company.

6 Draft copy can be used to check the hard copy against the printout for any errors and amendments made prior to printing full resolution print.

7 RAM stands for Random Access Memory.

8 To check that there is enough memory to produce your publication.

9 Text and graphics editor.

Section 2 Creating a master style

Practise your skills 3

Practise your skills 4

The Data Protection Act

The Data Protection Act of 1998 was created and identified eight principles of which data could be held.

The Principles say that:

1. fairly and lawfully processed;
2. processed for limited purposes;
3. adequate, relevant and not excessive;
4. accurate;
5. not kept for longer than is necessary;
6. processed in line with your rights;
7. secure; and,
8. not transferred to countries without adequate protection.

By law data controllers have to keep to these principles.

The Information Commissioner and his staff and his staff is to ensure that organisations that are processing data are doing so in line with the obligations that are placed upon them by the various pieces of legislation such as: the Data Protection Act, Freedom of Information Act and the Privacy and Electronic Communications Regulations.

This Act places obligations on data users to:

Register data held and usage with the Data Protection Commission

Hold data for only the purpose that it has been registered

Make the data available to the data subject on request

As an individual you can ask for a copy of any information held on you by an organisation. This is commonly known as "Subject Access Request".

Further information can be found on the Information Commission's Official Website

Check your knowledge

1 House styles are used to create standard publications which are consistent throughout an organisation.

2 A master page can be created and will offer consistent layout throughout multiple pages in a publication.

3 Creating a template allows you to create new publications based on the template so that they are consistent throughout the organisation or series of publications. A template also saves time.

4 When using colour you should consider how text/images will be produced on dark coloured backgrounds and the amount of ink that will be used.

5 The background is where headers/footers are created and shown on every page. Images can also be placed on the background.

Section 3 Working with text

Check your knowledge

1 (a) Rich text file

   (b) Text

   (c) Microsoft Word

2 Creating a text style produces a consistent layout and also makes it easier to change the style at a later date.

Section 4 Text layouts

Task 4.5

London

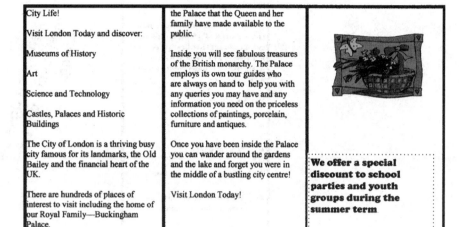

City Life!	the Palace that the Queen and her family have made available to the public.	
Visit London Today and discover:	Inside you will see fabulous treasures of the British monarchy. The Palace employs its own tour guides who are always on hand to help you with any queries you may have and any information you need on the priceless collections of paintings, porcelain, furniture and antiques.	
Museums of History		
Art		
Science and Technology		
Castles, Palaces and Historic Buildings		
The City of London is a thriving busy city famous for its landmarks, the Old Bailey and the financial heart of the UK.	Once you have been inside the Palace you can wander around the gardens and the lake and forget you were in the middle of a bustling city centre!	**We offer a special discount to school parties and youth groups during the summer term**
There are hundreds of places of interest to visit including the home of our Royal Family—Buckingham Palace.	Visit London Today!	
The Palace is open for a short time each year and you can visit parts of		

1   Candidate Name and Date

Practise your skills 1

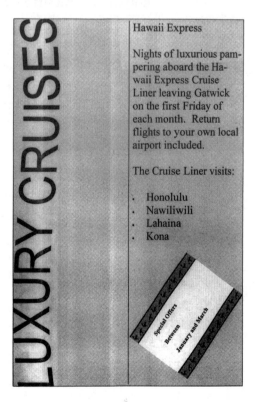

LUXURY CRUISES

Hawaii Express

Nights of luxurious pampering aboard the Hawaii Express Cruise Liner leaving Gatwick on the first Friday of each month. Return flights to your own local airport included.

The Cruise Liner visits:

- Honolulu
- Nawiliwili
- Lahaina
- Kona

Special Offers Between January and March

Practise your skills 2

Cars

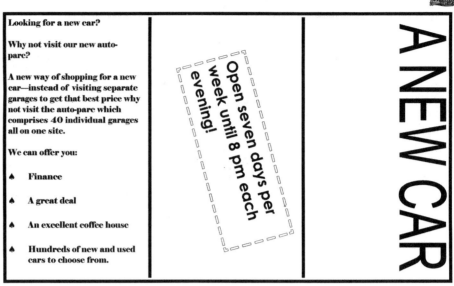

Candidate Name and Date

Check your knowledge

1 A callout box can be used to highlight certain words in the text.

2 Rotated text means that it has been moved around by a degree between 0 and 360.

3 Text density increases the emphasis of certain words.

4 A banner headline is a separate text frame which can be displayed differently to the body text and usually runs across the top of the page.

5 It is easier to create a text file as this uses less space on a disk.

Section 5 Text enhancements and formats

Task 5.2

The Cook Islands

The islands were named after Captain James Cook when he became the first European to see them. The main island, known as Rarotonga, became a British protectorate in 1888, and in 1901 became part of New Zealand, and was discovered by the Bounty Mutineers in 1789.

The best swimming beaches are at Muri Lagoon and Titikaveka. There is an excellent museum at Takamoa and a village tour allows you to see the locals demonstrating their weaving, coconut husking and carving.

The currency is the New Zealand dollar and there are plenty of currency exchanges available on the islands.

Task 5.3

Estonia is bordered by the Baltic Sea and the Russian Federation and Latvia and is a country of great scenic beauty with many forests, lakes and islands

Practise your skills 1

Internet Banking

Online or Internet banking offers you the main banking services with the ability to manage your investments and mortgages online.

Internet banking allows you to view balances and statements, you can transfer funds between accounts, pay bills and set up standing orders. If you have additional products such as credit cards, you can also check and repay any outstanding balances. One organisation allows you to add all your accounts to your portfolio which can all be viewed simultaneously once you have logged onto a secure area.

Some Internet Banking facilities were set up just to allow customers to bank online, however, many high street traditional banks now offer their customers this service allowing them to manage their finances without visiting the branch!

Updated 1st January

Practise your skills 2

What is Interior Design?

Our special Interior Design service specialises in the following areas and provides the following services:

- *Assessing the way the space will be used*
- *Calculating the dimensions of the space*
- *Identifying the significance of the space*
- *Considering, for example, light, acoustics or any special needs or disabilities to be catered for.*

$\mathcal{E}$lements of design include colour, shape, texture and noise and therefore our designer will see how you respond to these elements in order to provide you with the best designed space that you can live in for years to come!

$\mathcal{O}$ur designers have access to the latest fashion of furniture, fabrics, accessories and ornaments and will be able to show you examples of products that are available. Our catalogue covers the minimalist, the traditional, Victorian era and 21st century designs.

Our designer will provide you with plans within 48 hours of the first consultation!

Check your knowledge

1 (a) Bold – the heavy version of a particular font.

   (b) Italics – the sloped version of a particular font.

   (c) Roman – plain text.

   (d) Text with lines underneath.

2 A drop capital is usually used to highlight the start of a new story in column display.

3 A raised cap is usually a few lines deep above lines of text.

4 Strikethrough text has lines through it.

5 Subscript is below the line and superscript is above the line.

Section 6 Working with folders

Practise your skills 1

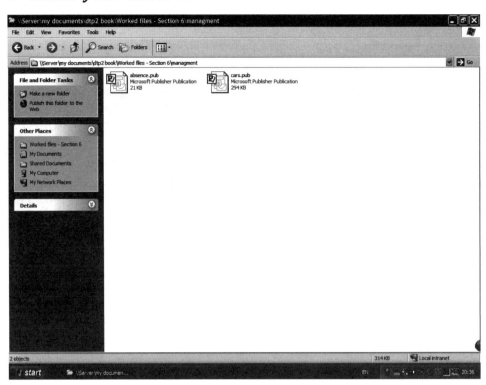

Practise your skills 2

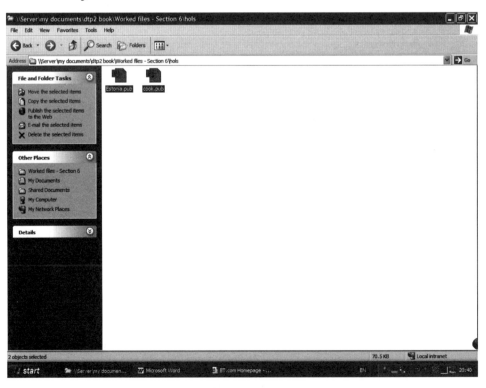

Practise your skills 3

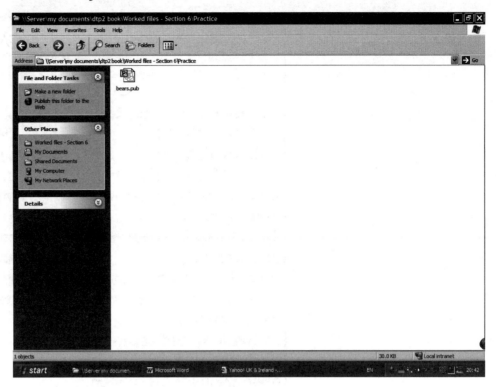

Check your knowledge

1 It is good practice to create folders as you can organise your files more effectively.

2 Moving files mean that they are moved from one location to another. Copying a file means that the file remains in the old location and another copy is created in the new location.

CHANGE FATIGUE

Too much change, too fast, too often!

Change fatigue can be caused by rapid change which has been poorly managed.

The change can cause uncertainty, demotivation and stress so individuals become demoralised.

Individual and team performance drops and absenteeism increases.

The fatigue results when the drivers for change, eg technology, new regulations or rulings, are uncoordinated and companies try to re-engineer themselves as quickly as possible in order to respond to customer needs but to drive costs down wherever possible.

Avoid Change Fatigue
- Evaluate and revisit corporate plans to make sure you are still on track
- Don't destroy old systems until the new ones are fully installed and staff are trained.

Remember your body needs to re-cover!

Section 7 Working with graphics

Practise your skills 1

Check your knowledge

1 A scanner is a piece of computer hardware used to capture paper-based text/images.

2 A scanner converts paper-based text and images into a digital format.

3 Vector images are picture formats and bitmap images are graphics, such as photos that you can change the size and shape of.

4 If an image has been created by someone else you need to get their permission before you can use it.

5 A graphics editor can be used to change the brightness/contrast and colours of images before being imported into Publisher.

6 The higher the resolution the better quality the printout.

JET AIRCRAFT

Aircraft

Emergency

Procedures

These procedures have been updated in line with consultation from both the UK and USA governments.

Practise your skills 2

FIRE RISKS IN HOTELS

This new publication has been produced to comply with recent changes in health and safety legislation and will help you to assist our customers, should a fire start.

Check your knowledge

1 Anchoring images means that when any amendments are made to the publication the image and text will move together.

2 Using the layout/grids allows you to align pictures and text frames consistently and behave as a template.

3 Two fill effects could be pattern or gradient fills.

4 Brightness is the number of shades shown on an image. Contrast determines the intensity of the shades of colour.

Section 9 Attributes or properties of an image

Task 9.3

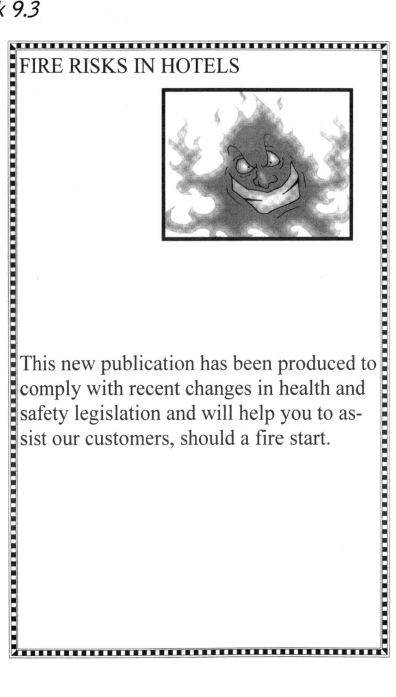

FIRE RISKS IN HOTELS

This new publication has been produced to comply with recent changes in health and safety legislation and will help you to assist our customers, should a fire start.

Task 9.5

ADOPT A LION

Today you can adopt a lion for less than £1 per day.

Lions are disappearing so fast from parts of Africa they could soon become extinct. As farming spreads throughout west and central Africa, the World Conservation Union says lions' habitats are disappearing fast but the big cats are also being killed off by poisoning and hunting which is still legal in some countries.

Your adoption helps towards the upkeep of the animal so if you have always wanted to look after a Lion but were afraid it would eat the cat, this is the next best thing!

Contact us today for further information!

Task 9.6

Special Gifts

Looking for that unusual gift? Why not consider theatre tokens?

Drama tokens are welcomed at over 210 theatres nationwide including those in the West End allowing you to choose what you want to see, when and where.

You can choose from classical ballet, comedy, dramas and blockbuster musicals.

Theatre tokens are available in £1, £5, £10 and £20 denominations and have no expiry date.

INTERNET CAFÉ

Our new internet café is open 7 days a week between the hours of 10 am and

10 pm.

Each computer is linked up via Broadband allowing high

speed access and costs just £2 for 20 minutes of access.

Strict terms and conditions must be adhered to and these will be provided on re-

quest.

Our dedicated staff are trained to provide help and support and we have a tech-

nician on site should problems occur.

Why not visit us and find out

more!

Check your knowledge

1 Wrap text frame is where images are wrapped 'square' against an image whereas irregular text wrap is where the text wraps in an irregular shape around the image.

2 A picture resized not in proportion would be distorted.

3 To create an interesting display or if you have a lot of text and want your publication to fit onto one page.

4 Flipping an image would make it visible as if you were looking at it through a mirror.

Section 10 Copyfit the publication

Task 10.2

Special Gifts

Looking for that unusual gift? Why not consider theatre tokens?

Drama tokens are welcomed at over 210 theatres nationwide including those in the West End allowing you to choose what you want to see, when and where.

You can choose from classical ballet, comedy, dramas and blockbuster musicals.

Theatre tokens are available in £1, £5, £10 and £20 denominations and have no expiry date.

Task 10.4

INTERNET CAFÉ

Our new internet café is open 7 days a week between the hours of 10 am and 10 pm.

Each computer is linked up via Broadband allowing high speed access and costs just £2 for 20 minutes of access.

Strict terms and conditions must be adhered to and these will be provided on request.

Our dedicated staff are trained to provide help and support and we have a technician on site should problems occur.

Why not visit us and find out more!

Practise your skills 1

Property of the Week

Would you like to live in a Grade II listed cottage with thatched roof and original features? We have the ideal property for you.

The property features a long drive leading up to the front of the property with large solid wooden gates which provide a secure garden and off road parking. A single garage with up and over door is provided next to the property which features a fenced area of lawn, a pergola over decking crossing the village stream and paved courtyard.

The property has accommodation on two floors and on entering the property you find yourself in the sitting room which features an inglenook fireplace over a flagstone hearth. The inglenook has space for a log store, seating and a small shelved open cupboard. The beams are exposed to the ceiling and there is a large window featuring a window seat. Double doors lead into the dining room with fireplace and views across the village green.

The kitchen and breakfast room provide built-in pantry with larder and the utility room houses the washing machine and dishwasher and access to the loft area, and a stable door to the rear garden.

The master bedroom has a high ceiling into the eaves and exposed crossbeams. The original bedroom door opens into a dressing room with built in wardrobes and there is an en-suite bathroom and access to the loft space. Two further bedrooms have similar high ceilings and share a family bathroom.

Check your knowledge

1 Symmetry means that it is centred.
2 Leading is the space between lines.
3 Kerning is the space between each character.
4 Publications look more professional without hyphenation.
5 You should plan white space in your publication to make the publication easier to read and allow text/images to be displayed more effectively.

Gulet Boats

Why not cruise around Crete in a stylish Gulet Boat?

These boats are spacious with four air conditioned cabins, with double beds and each with en-suite facilities.

The boats include a lounge area away from the rays of the sun with a comfortable dining area on the front deck.

The boats can be hired with a crew of four including a captain to make your cruise extra special!

Once on board you can enjoy our extra facilities of a motorboard, canoe or windsurfing!

Section 11 Colour separation

Check your knowledge

1 CMYK stands for Cyan, Magenta, Yellow and Black.

2 The pantone matching system uses a numbering system for each colour and a swatch book is available for you to check the colours. The chart can be printed from Publisher.

3 Focoltone is a colour matching system.

4 Spot colour is used to separate the ink colour and print it on its own plate.

5 Where the original manuscript is set into type.

6 The differences arise because a monitor uses the RGB colour system and the printer uses CMYK.

Section 12 Print and file output considerations

Practise your skills 1

Property of the Week

Would you like to live in a Grade II listed cottage with thatched roof and original features? We have the ideal property for you.

The property features a long drive leading up to the front of the property with large solid wooden gates which provide a secure garden and off road parking. A single garage with up and over door is provided next to the property which features a fenced area of lawn, a pergola over decking crossing the village stream and paved courtyard.

The property has accommodation on two floors and on entering the property you find yourself in the sitting room which features an inglenook fireplace over a flagstone hearth. The inglenook has space for a log store, seating and a small shelved open cupboard. The beams are exposed to the ceiling and there is a large window featuring a window seat. Double doors lead into the dining room with fireplace and views across the village green.

The kitchen and breakfast room provide a built-in pantry with larder and the utility room houses the washing machine and dishwasher and access to the loft area, and a stable door to the rear garden.

The master bedroom has a high ceiling into the eaves and exposed crossbeams. The original bedroom door opens into a dressing room with built in wardrobes and there is an en-suite bathroom and access to the loft space. Two further bedrooms have similar high ceilings and share a family bathroom.

Check your knowledge

1 The proofing process allows you to check your publication for errors and to make sure that all items are displayed accurately.

2 You need to consider whether you are using TrueType fonts and whether these should be embedded into your publication so that they can be used by a professional printing company.

3 Crop marks are small lines that are used to show the custom size of documents printed on any size of paper.

Practice Assignment

Task A

DESIGNONLINE.COM—TODAY'S DATE

Task B

NEW FOR SPRING/SUMMER

Our new internet catalogue is now available and we are pleased to announce that we have increased our ranges and now can exclusively offer to you men's and childrenswear. As always our products offer exceptional quality, modern styling at extremely affordable prices!

Our men's and ladieswear designs have been specially created to ensure that each item offers you quality and design that you have come to expect.

Childrenswear

Our new childrenswear section includes those new additions to your family and teenagers who are looking for the ultimate in high fashion quality clothing.

Menswear

Our new menswear section has everything you need for that man in your life! From workwear to casual/weekend wear and sports outfits offering our superb quality and affordability promise.

Designer Brands

Our designer brands have increased and we are pleased to announce three new designers. The designers have been showing their fashions round the world and have decided to settle in England and offer their designs via our company.

Stock and Purchasing

You can check whether the item you want is in stock when you shop online. Just click on an item or type in the catalogue number to find out and remember you can try the goods at home before agreeing to purchase!

Remember ordering is secure and goods can be with you within 24 hours of ordering your items.

Remember to order before 5pm and get free delivery within 48 hours or pay £4.99

for next day delivery (except Saturday and Sunday).

Regards
Designonline.com

Answers

1 This is to ensure your computer has enough memory to create your publication.

2 It would be easier, quicker and can be imported into Publisher.

3 The scanner resolution setting (dpi) makes a difference to each image scanned and the higher the dpi the bigger the image file stored.

4 (a) Cyan, Magenta, Yellow, Black.

   (b) DIC for focoltone.

   (c) Differences in colour may occur because the monitor is using three colours, RGB, whereas printed output can use four colours, CMYK.

5 One method can be to provide four colour prints offset without the images and indicating to the printer where the images should be placed.

6 The font can be increased/decreased without distorting the final effect.

Outcomes matching guide

	Outcome 1: Use the DTP system environment to produce output combining and manipulating data from a variety of outcomes	
Practical activities The candidate will be able to:		
1	Select suitable system hardware for DTP • Random Access Memory (RAM) • monitor (VDU) • mouse • keyboard • hard disk • floppy disk • CD-ROM • printer	Section 1 Section 1 Section 1 Section 1 Section 1 Section 1 Section 1 Section 1
2	Use the operating system to manage directories/folders and files	Section 6
3	Use a word processor or text editor to create, edit and save a text file	Section 3
4	Use a graphics editor to edit and save a graphic file	Section 7
5	Import text and graphics into a new DTP file	Sections 8, 9, 10
6	Save a DTP file to a specified location	Section 1
Underpinning knowledge The candidate will be able to:		
1	Describe the reasons for checking the available memory (RAM) and storage space before creating DTP files	Section 1
2	Describe the reasons for importing elements of a DTP publication from different applications software	Section 1
3	Describe different text file formats • .rtf • .txt • word processor files	Section 3 Section 3 Section 3
4	Describe different graphic file formats and copyright issues that may arise from their use • .gif • .tif • .jpeg • .bmp • vector	Section 7 Section 7 Section 7 Section 7 Section 7

Outcome 2: Set up a publication layout		
Practical activities		
The candidate will be able to:		
1	Set up a master style in a given house style	
	• margins	Section 2
	• gutters	Section 1
	• backgrounds	Section 2
	• colour	Section 2
	• page orientation	Section 1
2	Create a multi-page document using a housestyle	Section 2
3	Insert running items into a multi-page document	
	• headers to include a positioned title	Section 2
	• footers to include page numbering	Section 2
4	Select suitable colours and produce them on the screen by specifying the colour components	Sections 11, 12
5	Set columns on a master page for a multi-page document	Section 2
6	Save the publication layout (template/master) so it may be used for different documents	Section 2
Underpinning knowledge		
The candidate will be able to:		
1	Describe the purpose and role of house styles	Section 2
2	Identify basic principles and means of ensuring effective communication using printed images	
	• use of white space	Section 10
	• use of rules	Section 10
	• page layout and use of grids	Section 2
	• symmetry/asymmetry	Section 10
	• use of colour	Section 8
3	State the impact of methods of binding multi-page documents on page layout	
	• margins	Section 4
	• gutters	Section 4
4	Describe the reasons for using 'rules and borders' in headers and footers	Section 4
5	State reasons why differences in colour may arise between the screen, colour proofs and the final printed output	Section 11
6	Describe in simple terms means of creating reproducible colours using colour component models	
	• RGB (red, green, blue)	Section 11
	• CMYK (cyan, magenta, yellow, black)	Section 11
7	Describe a pre-defined colour scheme commonly used to specify colours for two-colour printing	
	• pantone matching system	Section 11
	• DIC	Section 11
	• focoltone	Section 11
8	Describe the reasons for saving a publication layout in a format suitable for multiple future use	Section 4

Outcome 3: Manipulate text		
Practical activities The candidate will be able to:		
1	Use guides or page layout grids to position and align text	Section 8
2	Use different text layouts • line and character spacing • bullet and numbered lists • indents/hanging indents • side headings • rotated/skewed text • banner headlines • callout boxes • justification	Section 10 Section 4 Section 4 Section 2 Section 4 Section 4 Section 4 Section 1
3	Use different text enhancements and formats • font • font size • bold, italics, roman • dropped and raised capitals • reverse text • tinted backgrounds • leading • kerning • hyphenation • underline • strikethrough • subscript, superscript	Sections 1, 5 Sections 4, 5 Section 5 Section 5 Section 5 Section 8 Section 10 Section 10 Section 10 Section 5 Section 5 Section 5
4	Use interline and character spacing, leading, pair kerning and hyphenation to fit copy to a given space	Section 10
5	Create and use different text styles	Section 4
6	Save the publication to a specified location	Section 6
Underpinning knowledge The candidate will be able to:		
1	Identify basic principles and means of ensuring effective communication using printed images • typefaces and typesetting • type: layout, structure, emphasis • illustration • page layout grids • guides	Sections 1, 10 Sections 4, 5 Section 10 Section 2 Section 2
2	Describe the purposes of using different text layout designs when creating a publication • text density • white space • special text effects • wrap • rotated and skewed text	Section 4 Section 10 Section 5 Section 9 Section 4

3	Describe the purposes of selecting different typographical designs when creating a publication	
	• serif	Section 1
	• sans serif	Section 1
	• roman	Section 5
	• italic	Section 5
	• upper case, lower case	Section 5
	• tinted backgrounds	Section 8
	• dropped and raised capitals	Section 5
	• describe the reasons for creating text styles	Section 4
4	Distinguish between printer and screen fonts and bitmap and scaleable fonts	Section 12

Outcome 4: Manipulate graphic objects

Practical activities
The candidate will be able to:

1	Use a scanner or digital camera to capture an image and import it into a graphics editing application	Section 7
2	Use the facilities of a graphic editing programme with a bitmap image imported from file to adjust the brightness and contrast of the image	Section 8
3	Use guides or page layout grids to position and align graphic elements on pages containing text	Section 8
4	Anchor a graphic image to a specified position	Section 8
5	Change the attributes/properties of a graphic object	
	• size	Section 9
	• position	Section 9
	• shape	Section 9
	• border	Section 9
	• background	Section 9
6	Apply flip/mirror, scale, rotate and crop to a graphic object	Section 9
7	Add a frame to a graphic image	Section 9
8	Add a caption to a graphic image	Section 9
9	Wrap text around a graphic image	Section 9
10	Combine text and a graphic image to produce text over the image	Section 9
11	Edit a graphic image to modify the colour, fill colour and style	Section 9
12	Save the publication to a specified location	Section 6

Underpinning knowledge
The candidate will be able to:

1	Describe scanners and their use as an input device to transfer paper based documents into electronic format	Section 7
2	Describe how a graphics editor can be used to undertake pixel editing and to	Section 7
	• change the fill colour or style	Section 7
	• add to the image	Section 7
	• delete from the image	Section 7

3	State that DTP software is able to recognise and import (or convert) most common graphic files	Section 7
4	Describe the difference between vector (line) and bitmap (dot) methods of producing images	Section 7
5	Describe how resolution settings affect the level of detail of an image	Section 12
6	Describe the benefits of anchoring text and/or graphic images in a particular position	Section 9

Outcome 5: Produce printed and file output

Practical activities
The candidate will be able to:

1	Use the application preview facility to view and check that output is suitable for printing	Section 12
2	Use an A4 output device to produce small-scale versions of a complete document to show the layout used	Section 12
3	Use an A4 output device to produce an A5 document with registration and crop marks	Section 12
4	Produce final output to specifications • no copies • resolution • size • monochrome • colour	 Section 12 Section 12 Section 12 Section 12 Section 12
5	Save printed output to disk	Section 6

Underpinning knowledge
The candidate will be able to:

1	Describe printer fonts • soft (downloadable) • resident (built in or internal) • scaleable	 Section 12 Section 12 Section 12
2	Explain the reasons for the proofing process	Section 12
3	Describe suitable electronic formats for storing printed output	Section 12
4	Describe the characteristics, uses and weights of commonly used types of paper	Section 1
5	Describe printing methods suitable for volume printing of documents such as magazines or books, eg two-colour and four-colour offset litho	Section 12

Quick reference guide

Action	Button	Menu	Keyboard
Arrows	⇄		
Bring to front			
Bold	**B**	Format, Font, Font style	Ctrl + B
Cancel			Esc
Centre align	≡		Ctrl + E
Character spacing		Format, Character spacing	
Close or Exit	⊠	File, Close or Exit	Alt + F4
Columns		Arrange – Layout guides	
Copy		Edit, Copy	Ctrl + C
Crop			
Cut	✄	Edit, Cut	Ctrl + X
End of line			End
Exit or Close		File, Close or Exit	Alt + F4
Fill – colour/ patterns		Format, Text Box	
Flip/mirror			
Font	Times New Roman ▾	Format, Font	
Font colour	A.	Format, Font, Color	
Font size	12 ▾	Format, Font, Size	
Go to background/ foreground		View, Master Page	Ctrl + M
Gutter		Format, Text Box	
Insert clip art		Insert, Picture, ClipArt	
Insert picture		Insert, Picture, From File	
Italics	*I*		Ctrl + I
Justify	≣		Ctrl + J

Left align	≡		Ctrl + L
Line/Border style	≡		
Line colour	✎		
Line spacing		Format, Line spacing	Ctrl + 1 Ctrl + 2 Ctrl + 3 (1.5 line space)
Margins		Arrange, Layout Guides	
New publication	▯	File, New	Ctrl + N
Open file	◻	File, Open	Ctrl + O
Paper size/ orientation		File, Page Setup	
Paste	▤	Edit, Paste	Ctrl + V
Print	▤	File, Print	Ctrl + P
Print to file		File, Print, click on Print to file	
Redo	↻	Edit, Redo	
Right align	≡		Ctrl + R
Rotate		Format Text Box, Text Box	
Ruler guides		Hold shift down, drag from ruler	
Save	▤	File, Save	Ctrl + S
Save As		File, Save As	F12
Select all (in a text frame)		Edit, Select All	Ctrl + A
Send to back	▤		
Spellcheck	✓	Tools, Spelling	F7
Start of line		Home	
Transparent fill			Ctrl + T
Underline	U	Format, Font, Underline	Ctrl + U
Undo	�undo	Edit, Undo	

Upper case		Format, Font, All Caps	
View options	50% ▾ ⊖ ⊕	View, Zoom	
Zoom	50% ▾ ⊖ ⊕	View, Zoom	F9